"What a Week!"

Simon exclaimed, pulling her gently down beside him. "Do you realize that I haven't had two minutes alone with you?"

"But it's been a good week in some ways," she said quickly, knowing exactly what was on his mind. "I've made a lot of progress with Katie."

"There speaks the good doctor," Simon said dryly. "I wonder if you know how chilling it is when you don your white coat—metaphorically speaking, that is. You always feel safer bringing our discussions back to my daughter. Who is it you don't trust, Carol? Me, or yourself?"

DIANA DIXON
loves to travel, both in the U.S. and in Europe. But she says that her real inspiration comes from "eighteen years of happy marriage to a man who gets more handsome with the passing years."

Dear Reader:

Silhouette has always tried to give you exactly what you want. When you asked for increased realism, deeper characterization and greater length, we brought you Silhouette Special Editions. When you asked for increased sensuality, we brought you Silhouette Desire. Now you ask for books with the length and depth of Special Editions, the sensuality of Desire, but with something else besides, something that no one else offers. Now we bring you SILHOUETTE INTIMATE MOMENTS, true romance novels, longer than the usual, with all the depth that length requires. More sensuous than the usual, with characters whose maturity matches that sensuality. Books with the ingredient no one else has tapped: excitement.

There is an electricity between two people in love that makes everything they do magic, larger than life—and this is what we bring you in SILHOUETTE INTIMATE MOMENTS. Look for them wherever you buy books.

These books are for the woman who wants more than she has ever had before. These books are for you. As always, we look forward to your comments and suggestions. You can write to me at the address below:

Karen Solem
Editor-in-Chief
Silhouette Books
P.O. Box 769
New York, N.Y. 10019

DIANA DIXON
Quest for Paradise

Silhouette Special Edition

Published by Silhouette Books New York

America's Publisher of Contemporary Romance

Other Silhouette Books by Diana Dixon

Return Engagement
Mexican Rhapsody
Gamble of Desire
Jessica: Take Two

SILHOUETTE BOOKS, a Simon & Schuster Division of
GULF & WESTERN CORPORATION
1230 Avenue of the Americas, New York, N.Y. 10020

Distributed by Pocket Books

ISBN: 0-671-53599-4

First Silhouette Books printing June, 1983

10 9 8 7 6 5 4 3 2 1

Map by Ray Lundgren

America's Publisher of Contemporary Romance

Printed in the U.S.A.

Quest for Paradise

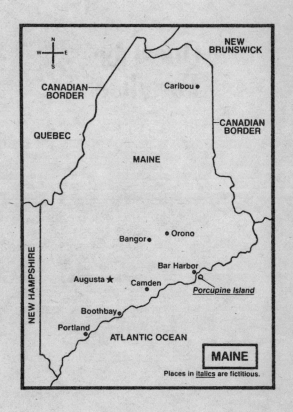

Places in _italics_ are fictitious.

Chapter One

*T*he setting sun had turned the Charles River to a broad expanse of gold. The leaves had passed their peak a couple of weeks before, but a few tenacious maples held on to their red and yellow cover. Against the pale orange of the late afternoon sky, the buildings of downtown Boston rose in striking silhouette. Carol wished that Rick Sanders would give her a chance to enjoy the beauty of the Indian summer day, but he had other things on his mind. Purposefully she disengaged herself from his clinging arms.

"I've got to get home now, Rick."

"Come on, honey," he coaxed. "Say you'll go. I can finish my business in Hyannis by noon and we'd have all the rest of the weekend to play around."

Prudently Carol leaned her head back against the fine leather bucket seat of the Alfa-Romeo and stared straight ahead out the window, turning a blind eye to the engaging smile on Rick's handsome tanned face and the pleading in his dark brown eyes.

"The answer is still no, Rick."

His glance moved hotly over her face, away from the sleek ash blond hair pulled back into its usual chignon, down the smooth line of her slender neck, and came to rest on the full, lush curves of her breasts that not even the bulky cable-knit sweater could entirely obliterate. She glanced sideways, caught that burning look in those soulful eyes and looked quickly away.

"Come on, baby!" Rick moaned. "I need you so bad! Let me love you!"

"Please, Rick!" she pleaded as he reached out for her again. "Don't!"

"Please, Rick! Don't!" he mimicked. "That's all you've been saying to me for a month now! You'd think I was some hustler looking for a one-night stand. I want to marry you!"

Unconsciously Carol sighed. Rick's persistence was very wearing, and since she wasn't given to vanity, it still baffled her that he had singled her out for his ardent attention. They had little in common. He had no more tolerance for her busy, hardworking diligence than she had patience with his conscientious pursuit of idle pleasure. There were far more compatible women clamoring for his favor. In fact, he had only to raise one thick blond eyebrow to have half the female population of Boston groveling at his feet.

That was the problem, of course, Carol concluded shrewdly. His conquests came too easily. They lacked the sport of the chase. He had taken her refusal to engage in an affair as a challenge. But marriage was carrying the obsession to conquer a little too far!

No, she was being unfair to him. She had to believe him when he said he wanted her. Too often in the past weeks she had felt the urgency of his yearning for her, the trembling of his body against hers, but he aroused no passionate response in her. Because you don't love him, both her heart and mind affirmed.

Nervously she bit her lip. Maybe the kind of love she had hoped for didn't exist outside of fiction. After all, she had thought she loved Brian. . . .

"You're not listening to me!" Rick protested petulantly.

"I'm sorry, Rick," she murmured. Sorry I don't love you. Sorry I won't sleep with you, she continued silently.

"Do you know what I think?" he went on playfully. "I think too many men have let you have your own way for far too long. Didn't your mother ever teach you that a man doesn't like independent women? He needs a soft, cuddly little kitten who wants to be taken care of."

His tone was joking, but Carol caught the steel behind his words—steel, censure, and a chauvinism that made her wince.

"Would you take me home now, please?" she asked quickly, before she could make a scathing response. She was too tired now for a full-scale battle. "You know Arthur is picking me up in an hour, and I've got to change."

"Forget about the old buzzard, sweetheart!" he protested. "Let him go to the exhibit alone. *I* need you! And I want you to myself tonight. My God, you see him all day long!"

"He's my boss and my friend," she reminded him coldly. "He doesn't often ask for my time outside of office hours, but tonight is a command performance."

"When are you going to quit that stupid job?" Rick demanded with the first outward show of irritation. "It's not as though you needed the money!"

The comment reconfirmed Carol's conviction that marriage to Rick would be a tragic mistake. She might enjoy his companionship and the fun they had together, but her work provided her with tremendous satisfaction, self-esteem and a sense of purpose. She had worked hard in her profession—too hard to give it up. And she knew that if she married Rick, he would never allow her to work.

Allow! Her use of the word rang danger bells in her head. She had been independent too long to consider giving any man the right to make her decisions for her.

"Will you take me home now, please?" she asked again, more coldly this time.

Rick's muttered oath did not surprise her. His growing impatience was reaching the crisis stage. She glanced quickly at his face and noted that the good-natured charm had faded. For just a moment she had a disquieting glimpse of the man behind the smile, a man she had never seen before and was quite sure she did not like at all.

Inwardly she sighed, dreading the confrontation with Rick that had to come soon. It wasn't fair to keep him dangling and hoping, and the strain on her nerves was beginning to tell.

"Rick, I'm going to be late!"

His mouth clamped shut into a stubborn, unpleasant line at the irritation in her voice.

"Rick!" she repeated in exasperation.

"What if I won't take you home?" he asked curtly.

"Then I guess I would have to get out and walk."

"I guess you could do that, couldn't you!"

"Am I going to have to?" she asked tartly.

"Women don't walk away from me, Carol!"

She knew he was furiously angry with her, but she wasn't exactly pleased with him at that moment herself. "Well, there always has to be a first time for everything, doesn't there?" she snapped.

"Is that a challenge?" A flush was creeping up his neck.

"If you want to take it that way!"

A tense silence ensued, and Carol was the first to break under the strain. "I'm sorry, Rick. I don't want to quarrel with you now. I really do need to get home."

The apology seemed to mollify him a little, and some of his color faded. The smile was back on his face, though she noted that it did not reach his eyes.

"Just five more minutes," he said softly. "We belong together. Let me convince you." He took her wrist with one hand and worked his fingers up the inside of her sleeve. The other hand began to gently caress her knee. "I don't like quarreling with you either, honey. Give me a little kiss to show me just how sorry you are."

Reluctantly she turned her face to his and felt the familiar touch of his lips—hot, wet, seeking. Expertly he tried to manipulate her responses, forcing her lips apart, molding his mouth to hers, until with a groan he pulled her into his arms and his embrace became harder, more ardent. She squirmed uncomfortably until he pulled her head down on his shoulder and buried his face in her neck.

"Come to Hyannis with me this weekend," he murmured huskily, ignoring her resistance. "I want you so badly!"

He could not ignore the sudden hard pressure of her hands against his chest, and slowly he drew away, anger gathering on his face once again.

"Take me home," she sighed wearily. "You simply don't understand! I just can't make the kind of commitment you want!"

For a moment she thought he was going to protest, but instead he turned the key, and the powerful engine roared into life. He jammed the car into reverse and left a layer of rubber on the road as he squealed onto the street.

"Well, don't take your frustrations out on the car," she muttered through clenched teeth a few minutes later when he took a corner on two wheels and slammed on the brakes to avoid a jogger.

"And you're such an expert on sexual frustration, of course," he bit out, speeding past a line of traffic, whipping around another corner into a quiet residential street and screeching to a halt before the brownstone town house Carol shared with her aunt.

"Rick—" she began.

"No, don't say anything," he said stiffly. "I realize that now I'm the one who owes *you* the apology."

"I don't want an apology, Rick, but I think it might be better if we stopped seeing so much of each other."

Shock, anger and chagrin mixed on his handsome face. "You don't mean that!"

"Believe me, I do! You're asking more from me than I'm prepared to give, and to go on as we are wouldn't be fair to either of us. It would be better—"

"No, don't say any more now, Carol!" Rick interrupted quickly. "I've made you angry, and I'm sorry."

"But—"

"No, wait! You're right. We've got to stop this stupid playing around and get serious. Look, we can't talk now. I'll pick you up at the gallery tonight. What time will you be through?"

"Rick, I don't think—"

"You *owe* me this, Carol," he said harshly.

He was right, of course, Carol admitted. Oh, why had she allowed herself to become so involved with him? Because he had helped heal her bruised ego after Brian's betrayal, she acknowledged ruefully. He had returned to Boston and sought her out when her self-confidence had been at its lowest ebb.

"Carol?"

"All right, Rick," she sighed, reaching for the door handle. "We should be through by nine. You can pick me up then."

She felt a tremendous relief as she climbed the front steps. The decision had been made, and tonight she would put an end to the whole episode.

She wouldn't have felt so happy if she had looked back at Rick's face. His eyes watched her disappearing figure with an anger and a desire that flooded his face with color.

No woman, he thought harshly, had ever rejected him, and Carol was not going to be the first!

The small, exclusive gallery just off Beacon Street was crowded to overflowing with the cream of Boston society—a tribute to Simon Forbes's popularity as both a sculptor and a personality. In the first half hour of the opening of the art event of the season, the limited editions of the smaller works had sold to private collectors for enormous amounts and the larger pieces of bronze statuary had been tagged with the names of public galleries and renowned private institutions.

This was the first showing of Forbes's work in nearly two years, and the invited assemblage of wealthy patrons of the arts, critics and reporters had dressed for the occasion. Formally garbed waiters moved silently and efficiently through the crowd with trays of champagne and hors d'oeuvres. Flashbulbs popped as the rich and famous were captured examining various pieces of bronze art.

Groups formed amoebalike around a particular sculpture, conversed, separated and then re-formed into new configurations. Conversations were punctuated with exclamations of awe, appreciation and reverence from the knowledgeable, high shrill giggles of embarrassment from the younger set and not a few murmurs of disgust and disapproval from the older generation.

But no one, Carol mused, viewed Simon Forbes's work with indifference—a fact, she supposed, that had made him the colorful and highly controversial artist that he was.

She and Arthur French stood to one side at the back of the crowd that had congregated around the major work of this new exhibit, a bronze statue that was some eight feet in height. *Cleopatra with Asp* depicted the Egyptian queen astride a giant, stylized serpent that twisted and encircled her nude body, its forked tongue just touching her parted lips. Cleopatra evidently embraced death with a wanton pleasure. Her body arched against the scaly skin of her reptile lover, her head was thrown back in sensual abandon and her hands molded the serpent's head in a fierce, pagan caress.

Carol found it impossible to look away from the expression of ecstasy on the queen's face. The bronze eyes under half-closed lids seemed to glitter with life. In her humble judgment the artistry of the piece was brilliant. The workmanship was modern, yet intricate in detail. The thrust of the piece seemed to be threatening, a violent movement that almost made one recoil in fear, yet the total created a startling, erotic tension that was breathtaking.

Slowly she expelled a breath she didn't know she had been holding. "Whew!"

"Like it?" her elderly companion asked with a smile.

"I'm not sure one can *like* a piece like that!" she answered honestly. "It's too—too elemental. It would be like asking if a person likes lightning. One can be awestruck by it, excited, stimulated, threatened—but like it?"

"Not unlike Simon Forbes himself," Arthur mused absently. "I'm pleased that you have the perception to see that."

Carol turned to look at the white-haired psychiatrist. The shrewd, assessing quality of his brilliant black eyes belied the soft pink and white complexion and ready smile. "Arthur, what are we doing here?"

His eyes moved with honest appreciation over Carol's slightly flushed face, took in the honey brown eyes, small straight nose and firm chin and proceeded downward over her slim figure. The cream-colored silk dress she wore suited her pale blond beauty to perfection. It was cut just low enough to reveal the curving tops of her high firm breasts, gathered flatteringly into her small waist and then fell in graceful folds down the length of her long legs. She looked lovely—warm, sophisticated, and very poised.

"Would you believe that it does wonders for my

ego to be seen in the company of such a stunning young woman?" he suggested with just the hint of a wicked gleam in his eyes.

"There's nothing wrong with your ego," Carol returned dryly, thinking of the petite, attractive fortyish widow who had been Arthur's companion for the past few months.

"Is that the woman or the psychologist in you speaking?" he asked whimsically.

"Either you're fishing for compliments or you're trying to lead me off the track!" she retorted sternly. "Now, what are we really doing here?"

"You don't admire Forbes's work?"

"Did you bring me to see his work or Forbes himself?" she countered shrewdly.

"You're far *too* perceptive," Arthur muttered.

"Which is why you hired me, remember? How about some straight answers?"

"All right," Arthur sighed. "I wanted you to see Simon's work first, and then when the crowd thins a little, I'll introduce you."

"Simon?" she asked curiously. "You know him that well?"

"I met him a little over a year ago."

"Privately or professionally?"

"Professionally," the doctor said tersely.

Carol knew enough from his tone not to press him further, but now her curiosity was really aroused. Arthur French had an international reputation as a psychiatrist, but he specialized in emotionally disturbed children. Carol had first met him three years before when he had been conducting workshops at the midwestern university where she had been finishing her Ph.D. in clinical psychology. A month previously an article she had written on the use of creative drama as therapy with children had appeared in a leading psychology journal, and Arthur had asked for an introduction. An invitation for her to join the select group of experts at his Boston clinic followed. Her professional success had been assured, but more than that, she loved her work, and in Arthur she had found a friend.

"Carol Durand!" interrupted a voice from behind them. "Darling, I haven't seen you in simply ages! The Junior League has been nothing since you deserted us! Simply nothing! Are you still working in that dreary clinic? Caught you on TV last week. You were marvelous, of course, but the camera is so aging!"

Maida Pearson always did speak in exclamations, Carol thought ungenerously as she turned to greet her old acquaintance. She had certainly never considered Maida a friend.

"Hello, Maida. Nice to see you again." She smiled through gritted teeth as she uttered the polite social lie. "Let me introduce Dr. Arthur French, who runs that dreary clinic. Arthur, Maida Pearson."

"So nice to meet you, Dr. French!" Maida gushed, totally undaunted by the irony in Carol's tone. "Isn't the exhibit divine! And Simon Forbes! What a man! He even makes my Teddy here look insignificant! Isn't that so, Teddy?"

Teddy whoever-he-was simply grinned fatuously and reached for a glass of champagne from a passing tray.

"Brian was asking all about you," Maida was saying. "Did you know he was back in town, darling?"

Carol willed herself not to react and looked Maida straight in the eye. "No, I can't say I did. I haven't exactly kept track of him."

"Which all your friends can certainly understand," the other woman cooed maliciously. "You don't know, then, that he's married—the daughter of a fast-food king from Omaha. I'm sure Rick must be pleased to know that your ex-fiancé is out of the running. By the way, when are you going to put the poor boy out of his misery and set the date? It's certainly past time you married and rejoined the human race. So amusing! *You* giving other women advice on how to raise their children!"

"I'm afraid we must be going now, Carol," Arthur intervened quickly. "It certainly has been an experience meeting you, Miss . . . ?"

"Mrs. Pearson. But Mr. Pearson is long gone," Maida added airily.

"Which comes as a surprise to none of us," the doctor muttered as he took possession of Carol's arm and propelled her away from the woman.

"I take it you weren't charmed," Carol murmured, hating herself for allowing Maida to rile her so.

"God preserve me from neurotic women! Give me a disturbed child any day of the week!"

Arthur's irreverent condemnation of Maida Pearson did her heart good, and she put back her head and laughed. "Oh, Arthur! You are so good for my morale—"

She stopped abruptly as she raised her head and met the bright, interested gaze of a pair of dark blue eyes staring directly into hers.

Arthur followed the direction of her diverted attention and beamed his warm, encompassing smile. "Simon! I was hoping to catch you alone."

"I've just managed to give the reporters the slip for a moment."

He spoke to Arthur, but his eyes were still fixed on Carol's face. She had never met Simon Forbes, but the erotic art that was his specialty had captured the attention and imagination of the media, and his picture appeared with regularity in the newspapers and on the covers of popular magazines. But now, at close range, she saw that the camera did not do him justice. His height, breadth and dark virility seemed to defy reproduction.

"You've really outdone yourself with this showing," Arthur was saying.

"I'm glad you could make it. This is Dr. Durand?"

"Yes. Carol, Simon Forbes."

"Mr. Forbes," she murmured, finding it difficult to look away from the magnetic draw of his blue eyes.

"Carol."

His voice was deep and strong, but no stronger than the hand that gripped hers. Her own slim fingers were totally engulfed, and she could feel the hard knots of muscle in his palm. Unconsciously her eyes dropped to those long knotted fingers, and her first impression was that she had never seen anyone with such large thumbs. But of course, she thought dizzily, a sculptor worked with his thumbs, molding and shaping the clay.

"I'm perfectly willing to go on holding hands all evening," Simon drawled. "How about later on tonight?"

Carol started and flushed as she realized that she was still standing with her hand in his, long beyond the duration of a conventional handshake.

"I'm sorry," she said softly, pulling her hand free with a quick jerk and forcing herself to meet the amused gleam in his eyes. The humor in his face was contagious, and an answering smile curved her lovely lips. "I must be a little awe-struck. I've admired your work for some time."

Her smile was having its own effect on Simon, and the interest in his eyes sharpened. "So you like my work, do you? Just what about it appeals to you? Does it appeal to your prurient interest? Titillate your passionate nature? Excite your libido?" he asked hopefully.

"It's obvious that there's nothing suppressed in your libido, Mr. Forbes," she offered dryly, meaning every word.

An appreciative smile faded into a puzzlement that held just a hint of censure. "You didn't warn me about her, Arthur. Why?"

Carol glanced quickly from one man to the other. What did Simon mean by that comment? Had Arthur been discussing her with the man? In what context and for what purpose?

"You're about to be descended upon, Simon," Arthur said quickly, ignoring the question. "We'll say good-bye now."

"Mr. Forbes!" a woman barked imperiously,

her tight face-lifted smile bright with determination. "You must meet my daughter. She's one of your most devoted fans . . ."

"My public calls," Forbes murmured dryly for their ears alone. "A shrill, penetrating sound, impossible to ignore! We'll meet again, Carol." The certainty in his voice gave her an odd breathless feeling. "I'll talk to you later, Arthur."

He had turned to speak to his determined followers, but Carol knew that his penetrating blue eyes never left her as she and Arthur crossed to the far side of the room.

"Well, what do you think of the great man?" Arthur asked.

"Unusual," she offered inadequately, "and younger than I'd thought he was—at least from his pictures."

"Thirty-six," Arthur supplied. "Is that all?"

Carol detected more than a passing interest in his inquiry. An imp of mischief danced in his eyes, as though he had already noted her reactions to the artist—and his to her. She glanced back to where Forbes stood parrying questions. Even from a distance she could see the firm set of his jaw, the prominent lines that ran beside his nose, the sensual, expressive movement of his mouth. Before she could look away, he caught her eyes on him and favored her with a casual salute.

"Well?" Arthur prompted.

"He—he has an interesting face," she said lamely.

"Character. That's what I see in his face," he said firmly. "He's a man you can trust. He inherited the Forbes fortune while still a young man, but in less than ten years he's made a second fortune on the strength of hard work and ability alone."

Carol stopped so abruptly that Arthur nearly bumped into her. "What's this all about, Arthur? I know you take perverse delight in playing your secretive little games with me, but would you care to fill me in on the rules of this one?"

"All will be revealed in good time, my child," he replied kindly. "You kept three o'clock tomorrow free for me?"

"Yes," she said wearily, accepting the change of subject. No use trying to probe. He was a past master at evasion when he chose to use it.

"Good. Now, do you want to have one last look at Cleopatra before we call it a night?"

"Out of prurient interest or to titillate my passionate nature?" she asked dryly.

"Simon did get to you, didn't he?" Arthur chuckled appreciatively.

"Well, I think you might have warned me that he was such a . . . such a—"

"Yes?" Arthur prompted hopefully, his eyes alight with interest. "Such a what?"

Fortunately Carol was saved from having to answer. "You ready, sweetheart?" Rick asked from behind her.

"Yes," she replied quickly. "Arthur, you know Rick Sanders, don't you?"

"Yes. Hello, Sanders."

"Dr. French." Rick nodded deferentially, none of his previous feelings toward the man apparent in his voice or manner.

Hypocrite! Carol couldn't help thinking. "Shall

we go, Rick?" she said coldly. "I'll see you tomorrow, Arthur."

Rick's hand on her arm was possessive as he led her toward the door, but he paused just inside the entryway. "Look at this one!"

"This one" was a graphic sculpture, *Delilah Subduing Samson*. Strange that the erotic art had not made her uncomfortable in Arthur's presence, but did now in Rick's.

"You might look and take lessons," he suggested. "Now, there's a woman!"

Which said what about her? Carol wondered, both annoyed and offended, and she wasn't any happier when she felt Rick's hand on her back, working its way up her spine to the nape of her neck. The art works were obviously having an effect on *his* libido.

"Shall we go?" she repeated curtly.

"Yeah, let's get out of here! I want you to myself!"

Carol glanced at him warily and with a growing unease. He had leaned close to whisper in her ear, and she caught the very potent smell of whiskey on his breath. Now that she noticed, she realized that the flush on his face had little to do with the showing. He was still wearing the same slacks and sports coat he had had on that afternoon when he picked her up from the clinic, and she could only conclude that he had spent the intervening hours at his club.

"I'm ready," she replied stiffly, wanting to get the evening over with as quickly and gracefully as possible.

"You look tense, baby." He favored her with a

long, slow, intimate smile as he helped her into the car. "I know just what you need to relax you. Just leave it to good old Rick."

"Where are we going?" she asked a few minutes later as he turned the car onto Massachusetts Avenue and headed toward Cambridge.

"My apartment. We can talk undisturbed there."

"We could go to my place," she suggested hastily. "It's closer, and one of the maids will be up. She could fix us something to eat."

"I said undisturbed!"

She watched his jaw tighten, locking the now not-so-charming smile on his lips.

"I'm very tired, Rick," she returned firmly. "I don't want to stay long—"

"Nonsense! It's only nine."

His voice was a little overloud for the small space, and she began to wonder just how much he had had to drink. Obviously at least one too many.

"I think we had better go to my place," she tried again. There she could speak her piece quickly and send him on his way.

"Later, baby. Later."

Short of jumping out of the speeding car, she had no way of stopping him. Something was wrong with Rick, she was sure, and the liquor didn't explain it all. She sensed a recklessness about him, a determination that was very different from his usual easygoing manner.

At that moment, however, he turned to smile at her, and she relaxed a little. They had had some very good times together, and despite their differences, she still considered him a friend. She would have been quite content to have gone on seeing him if he hadn't been pushing her so hard, if he had shown a willingness to let things ride between them.

She turned her head and studied the smooth, regular planes of his face, the way the light from the street lamps turned his sun-bleached hair almost white, the ready smile, the dark soulful eyes that could so flatter a woman . . .

Character. That's what I see in his face. He's a man you can trust. Arthur's words. Why had his description of Simon Forbes popped into her mind just now? she wondered, a little startled. Was it that she looked at Rick and saw all that was lacking?

Brian had had the same brand of superficial charm and looks. She had been devastated when she discovered that her onetime fiancé would have been just as willing to marry a middle-aged hag possessed of her name and fortune as herself. What had made the affair worse was knowing that her entire social set had guessed that Brian was only pursuing her for her money. Supposed friends like Maida Pearson had watched with malicious delight while she made a fool of herself.

Some psychologist she had been!

The psychologist in her now, however, was definitely beginning to sense trouble as Rick drew up in front of the large brick house where his apartment comprised the entire second floor. The whole place was in darkness, and her unease grew as Rick flashed her that intimate smile once again and reached out to squeeze her hand in a tight, convulsive grip. Every ounce of feminine instinct she possessed urged her to be very wary, and she cursed herself for not having insisted on somewhere public for their showdown. But before she could voice another protest, Rick was on her side of the car, opening her door. It was small courtesies like this, she knew, that made him a favorite with her aunt Cora.

As he held out his hand to her impatiently, she hesitated just a moment longer, then shrugged. Perhaps it was better that what she had to say to him be said in private.

Inside the apartment he lifted the coat from her shoulders, pressed a kiss on the side of her neck and tossed the coat negligently aside.

"Make yourself comfortable," he said huskily, "while I fix us a drink."

"Nothing for me," she answered quickly. "I drank enough champagne at the exhibit."

"Nonsense." He smiled. "A gin and tonic will do you good."

The way he had of overriding her decisions was another thing about him that troubled her, she concluded as she watched him pour a large measure of gin into a glass. Her doubts about the wisdom of being there firmed as he swallowed a neat whiskey and poured himself a second.

When he moved to join her on the couch his eyes raked possessively over her slim form and she drew in a quick chagrined breath at the fire that burned there.

"Bottoms up!" he ordered curtly, draining his own glass in one gulp.

Carol took a tentative sip and shivered. The

drink was much too strong. She looked up and met his expectant eyes over the rim of the glass.

"Well? What are you waiting for?" he prodded.

"It's awfully strong. . . ."

"Just what you need tonight," he coaxed.

Carol tried to set the glass on the coffee table in front of her, but Rick pressed it back into her hand. "Come on," he wheedled. "Loosen up! One little drink isn't going to hurt you."

"I have to work in the morning, remember?" she replied lightly, trying to keep a rein on her mounting temper.

"Relax! I'll get you there on time."

"You'll get me there?"

He smiled, but the charm was gone. The movement of his lips now was more a leer. "Or you can call in sick. That will give us the whole day together."

His meaning was too clear to be misinterpreted. "I think I had better go *now,* Rick," she said firmly.

The hand that had been resting on hers began a gentle, sensuous caress. "Nonsense. You haven't even finished your drink."

"I'm not going to finish it," she replied with forced calm.

"Sure you are, baby! It's time you realized that old Rick knows what's best for you." His leering smile deepened as his hot eyes devoured her. "We're going to have a good time tonight, sweetheart. A real good time! Then, tomorrow, we'll tell everybody we're getting married."

"No, Rick!" she said sharply, but he wasn't even listening.

"I want you so much!" he groaned. "No woman has put me off as long as you have, and you're the first one I've ever wanted to marry!"

Carol carefully edged away from him, preparing to stand and put as much distance between them as possible. Rick was in a dangerous mood tonight, like a lion primed to spring. When she made the move to rise to her feet, he anticipated the action and pounced. In one swift movement he grabbed her around the waist and, with a growl of delight deep in his throat, tossed her back on the couch. Before she could regain her senses he had pinned her to the unyielding leather cushions with the weight of his body and smothered her lips under his.

"Rick, no!" she gasped when his lips slid from hers to fasten on the hollow at the base of her neck.

"Rick, yes!" he moaned. "You're mine, and I want you—now!"

"Well, I don't want you!" she gasped. "Not now or ever!"

"Sure you do, sweetheart," he murmured with totally unjustified confidence. "I'm going to make you love it!"

On a moan of passion his lips again took hers in a demanding kiss that deprived her of breath. The overheated room was stifling; his weight crushed the strength from her and the overpowering taste of him nauseated her. An accompanying dizziness brought a dangerous lethargy to her limbs and she lay passive for a moment, weak and trembling in his arms.

Rick mistook this faintness for surrender. With

a grunt of satisfaction he loosened his hold slightly and half rose to readjust his body to hers.

As his weight lifted she quickly caught her breath. Anger sent a sudden rush of adrenaline to her aid. Before he could lower himself to her once again she pushed against his chest with both hands. Luck was with her. She caught him off balance. His arms flailed wildly for a moment, trying to find a hold, and then, with a cry, he went sprawling, half onto the floor and half onto the coffee table. His hand flicked against the gin and tonic Carol had left there and the contents spilled down his front. Carol couldn't suppress the giggle that rose in her throat as an ice cube slid inside the open V of his shirt and he let out a cry of rage.

She didn't have time, however, to enjoy his well-deserved discomfiture for long. Before he could regain his feet and his composure she had to be off the couch and out of his reach. In a flash she moved, putting the width of the room between them.

Rage and chagrin warred on his handsome face as he stared at her through a drunken haze—and rage won. "You frigid bitch!"

Carol had been sustained so far by her sense of the ridiculous, but now all possible humor faded and an icy calm settled over her as she looked at his face, twisted and distorted with anger. How could she ever have thought him handsome? she wondered in amazement. Her voice was cold with her outrage as she confronted him.

"You're free to believe that if it suits your egotistical male pride. But believe me when I tell you that I never want to see you again!"

"You don't mean that!"

He lurched to his feet and Carol took another step backward, but she knew that the danger had passed. Rick could hardly stand.

"No? Try me! Come to the house and I'll have Hawkins slam the door in your face."

"You frigid—!"

"You're repeating yourself, Rick," she interrupted, "and that's boring. I think I'll be going now. I can't see that we have anything left to say to each other."

"I can see why Brian Castle dumped you!" he bit out nastily.

Carol had been in the process of putting on her coat, and just for a moment she paused to swallow a gasp of pain. "I think you've said *more* than enough, Rick. Why don't you quit while you're ahead?"

"I'm not through with you, Carol! You're not throwing me over!"

His eyes were losing a little of their glaze and Carol realized that he was sobering up fast. Time to make a hasty retreat. She picked up the keys to his car, which he had tossed carelessly on a table.

"I'm taking your car, Rick. I'll see that Hawkins has it back to you first thing in the morning."

He staggered toward her as she headed for the door. "I know how to handle sexually repressed females, Carol," he sneered. "You'll see! I'm going to make love to you until you cry for more. By the time I'm finished with you, you'll beg me to marry you!"

Her eyes were hard as stone as they slid from his disordered hair over his flushed face to the wet, sticky shirt clinging to his chest. A derisive smile curved her lips.

"You're quick to give other people labels, Rick. How about finding one for yourself? I suggest you take a good hard look in the mirror right now and try conceited fool on for size!"

Chapter Two

At two minutes to three the next afternoon, Carol slipped unobtrusively into Arthur's office as he spoke on the phone. She took a chair away from the bright light of the windows, because the events of the previous night had left her a wreck. During the long, sleepless night she had vacillated between disgust at Rick's behavior and fear that there was some truth in what he had said.

Had she become frigid?

She knew that Brian's betrayal had frozen something deep inside her that Rick had been unable to thaw. She had loved Brian so much! No, she corrected herself. She had been infatuated with the person she thought him to be. You can't love a person you don't really know. . . .

"You look like you've been run over by a truck!"

Arthur had finished his phone call and stood watching her as she sat lost in thought. Now his sharp comment brought a flush to her pale face. She had been afraid that all her careful makeup wouldn't cover the ravages of the previous night's fiasco.

"What have you been doing to yourself?" he persisted.

"You really know how to make a woman feel just great," she returned evasively.

She had averted her face and did not realize that Arthur had left his desk until she felt his soft fingers under her chin forcing her face around to his.

"You have dark circles under your eyes," he said gently.

"They're nothing."

"Now, shall I gracefully accept the fact that you don't wish to confide in me, or shall I follow my natural instincts and probe a little?"

The warmth and honest concern in his voice were nearly her undoing. She wanted to confide in Arthur—not only as a friend, but as a psychiatrist.

"Well?" he prompted.

"You don't like neurotic women, remember?" she said with forced lightness.

"You're a long way from neurotic, my dear. Unhappy, yes. Neurotic, no. Now, you were your own charming self when you left me last night. Something happened to you. What?"

For a moment she hesitated, not liking to burden him with her personal problems.

"Come on," he said gently, "let's have it."

"Arthur, do you think I'm . . . well, sexually repressed?"

His eyes narrowed as he read the genuine concern behind the question. "Am I right in assuming that young Sanders put that idea in your head?"

At first she shook her head in a quick negative; then she slowly nodded.

"And by sexually repressed, I assume you mean you didn't choose to sleep with him last night?"

Again she nodded, a rueful dip of her head.

"And now he's managed to make you take the blame for his wounded ego." A statement, not a question.

"He's been asking me to marry him for a month now. And then last night he said—"

"—that you're sexually repressed," he finished for her. His dark eyes examined her face with an objective male appraisal. "You're far too lovely— and, unfortunately, wealthy—not to be fair game for the wrong kind of man, Carol. But accept my opinion not only as a doctor but as a knowledge-able male that there's nothing wrong with you that won't solve itself when you fall in love with a man who deserves and appreciates you. You are a warm, loving, giving woman with depths of passion that have never even been tapped."

The conviction in his voice was a balm to Carol's bruised heart, and she smiled her first genuine smile of the day. "Thank you," she said softly.

"My pleasure. I wish all problems were so easily solved." He patted her hand and rose to his feet. "Now you can do me a favor. I need your expert opinion on a particular case of mine."

She and Arthur discussed cases often, but she could tell that this one was somehow special. "Anyone I know?"

"No. A girl of eight," he said as he returned to his place behind the desk and opened a case folder. "A little over a year ago her mother was killed in a freak accident and the child hasn't spoken since."

"Trauma? I assume you've eliminated the possibility of any physical problem."

"Yes. At first, the family wasn't terribly concerned. Then it became obvious that the shock of her mother's death went deeper than they had thought. They took her to the Boston Children's Hospital and were eventually referred to me."

"So what would you like me to do?" she asked.

Arthur teetered back in his black leather swivel chair, his fingertips pressed together. "The child has been living with her grandmother and aunt since the accident. We thought it better if she was removed from the place where her mother's death occurred. At the time I agreed that a completely different environment might bring about its own cure."

"But it didn't."

Arthur frowned. "No. The grandmother wouldn't consent to therapy. I hadn't seen the child for several months until her father brought her in again the day before yesterday, and in my opinion her condition has, if anything, deteriorated."

"And now?" Carol prompted.

"Now the father wants to take her back home again and the grandmother objects. She has even gone so far as to take the issue to the authorities. I've been asked to give my professional opinion in the case, but before I do, I would like you to see the girl."

"Of course," she said quickly. "When?"

"Now, if you don't mind."

Carol rose. "What's her name?"

"Katherine. She's called Katie."

Katie was sitting in one corner of the therapy room when Carol entered. One of Arthur's assistants was making a futile attempt to interest her in a baby doll.

"Good luck," he murmured as he gave up his place beside the child.

The little girl, Carol noted, was dressed expensively, if not tastefully, in a red knit dress that did nothing for her straight bony figure. Her dark brown hair had been curled in elaborate ringlets that hung down the sides of her head, almost totally concealing her too-thin face. As Carol sat down beside her Katie turned her head only slightly, gave her a cursory glance, totally devoid of any real interest, and then continued to stare unblinkingly at the opposite wall.

"Hello, Katie," Carol said softly. "My name is Carol."

She made no attempt to elicit a response from the child, but turned instead to a box of blocks that stood on the table in front of the couch. One by one she began stacking them with extreme care, seemingly oblivious of the girl. She stacked them until a final block sent them toppling over.

Not by so much as an involuntary flinch did Katie acknowledge what was going on. Systematically Carol picked up the fallen blocks and began to reconstruct her tower. Again the blocks tumbled. Again no response. It wasn't until the fourth attempt that she could see the child's eyelids flicker when she reached the height where the blocks had fallen before. Carol gave an inward sigh of satisfaction. At last a sign of response—slight though it was. She had just begun the procedure again when Arthur arrived.

"Hello, Katie," he said cheerfully. "I'm going to take Carol away with me for a minute, but I'll be back soon."

No response from the child.

"Well?" Arthur asked as he joined her on the couch in the privacy of his office.

"Severely withdrawn. I was able to get an involuntary response from her, but it took some doing."

Arthur studied her face carefully. "And what treatment would you suggest?"

Carol frowned. "She certainly needs more than just periodic therapy sessions at the clinic. She needs constant daily attention in familiar surroundings."

Arthur smiled in satisfaction. "Exactly what I thought! My recommendation is that she be placed in her father's custody and returned to her own home under the care and supervision of a qualified psychologist."

"Barb Johnson would do well," Carol suggested thoughtfully. "Unless you have someone else in mind. She's just about the best intern I've ever had."

"So I've noticed. I'm very impressed with her. In fact, I've already offered her a permanent job here."

Carol was startled. He had said nothing to her, and neither had Barb, which was very unusual. Ordinarily he asked her opinion before hiring anyone in her particular area of specialization.

"And someone for Katie?"

"Oh," he said offhandedly, "I thought you might be interested in taking her on as a private patient for a couple of months. You haven't had a vacation in over a year. The work would be interesting and challenging, but not all that demanding. Want to give it a try?"

He spoke so carelessly that for a moment Carol wasn't certain whether he was serious.

"You want *me* to go and live at Katie's home?"

"Why not? Didn't you like her, the poor little mite?" he asked whimsically.

"Well, of course I did! But—"

"But what? You said yourself that Barb was very competent. There's no reason why she can't take over your cases here for a while."

He saw the doubt in her eyes and laid his hand gently over hers. "I care a great deal about both Katie and her father," he said softly. "There's no one in the country who's better than you are in your field. And I'm thinking of you, too. You've been pushing yourself too hard, Carol. After you broke your engagement to Brian it was good therapy, but look what you've taken on this past year! A lecture tour, television appearances, a book out, not to mention a full case load here. You're going to break under the strain if you keep this up!"

Nervously Carol bit her lip. Was Arthur right? Was that why her judgment about Rick had been so faulty? Oh, she was tired. She had been living on nervous energy for much too long.

"Do you see?" Arthur persisted. "You're strung on wires. If you were my patient I'd order you to take a month's cruise, but I know you too well to think you could be happy being completely idle. But give yourself a change of scene, anyway. Take a break. Buy some breathing space so you can look at yourself—and your involvements with Brian and Sanders, too—more objectively. Put them in perspective."

"But—"

"No, don't answer yet. Take a little time to think it over. You can let me know in a couple of days. I won't pressure you. The decision is yours."

He rose. "Why don't you come with me now and let me introduce you to Katie's father? He's been waiting in the next room."

He opened the door of his private consulting room and allowed her to precede him; otherwise Carol would have seen the twinkle in his eyes. Katie's father stood with his back to them, staring out the window, his tall broad frame silhouetted against the bright October day. Quickly he turned around as he heard the door close behind Arthur, and Carol suppressed a gasp of surprise.

Katie's father was none other than Simon Forbes!

"I don't know why you're looking so surprised," he said dryly. "I told you we'd meet again."

The light from the window put half his face in shadow, making it difficult to read his expression. He had spoken with that half-teasing note, but she sensed the tension in him. Not a muscle in his body, taut beneath his corduroy suit, was relaxed.

"Carol's opinion supports my own," Arthur was saying. "I'll call Judge Price immediately. I see no reason why you can't take Katie home with you when you go tomorrow."

Simon's relief was palpable. He expelled a long breath, and then a frown creased his broad forehead. "And the therapy?" he asked curtly.

Neither man was looking at her, but Carol knew that she had suddenly become the subject of this conversation.

"I should have an answer for you in a couple of days."

Now Simon's full attention was on her and she felt the blue heat of his eyes. "I want to talk to you about this, Arthur!"

"If you would like me to leave—" she began.

"No, Carol. Stay," Arthur cut in quickly.

"You're creating a touchy situation, Arthur!" Simon warned him sharply. "Surely there's someone else—"

"I'm leaving!" Carol interrupted, wounded by Simon's obvious rejection of her.

"Carol, stay. Simon, you know I have Katie's

best interests at heart. I've told you that there's no one better for the job than Carol Durand!"

"I don't like it, Arthur," Simon said stubbornly.

"You don't like me, you mean!" Carol exclaimed.

The look he shot at her belied her statement.

"Simon," Arthur said persuasively, "I think I know how you feel, but you've got Katie to consider."

The two men exchanged a knowing glance and Carol looked in bewilderment from one to the other. What was the problem? Did Forbes think her too young, too inexperienced?

"Have you explained to Carol what the situation would be if she took Katie's case?" Simon said dryly.

"What situation?" she asked impatiently.

"The living conditions!"

"You—you don't live here in Boston?"

"I keep an apartment here, but my house is in Maine—off the coast of Maine, to be exact." His eyes were probing, assessing, as though he were trying to read her character in a single gaze. "If you come to live with us you would have to endure fairly primitive surroundings. There's no town on Porcupine Island. Visitors are rare. You'd be there during the worst season. Winter comes early, and there are times when the sea is too rough to allow access to the mainland."

He was painting a very bleak picture. If he was trying to discourage her from taking the case he was doing a very good job.

"Sometimes during a nor'easter," he continued ruthlessly, "the wind blows down the power lines and knocks out the electricity from the generator. There's no telephone, only shortwave radio. We're practically cut off from civilization—"

"Simon!" Arthur expostulated, a hint of laughter in his voice.

Forbes shrugged, but gave the doctor a rueful smile. "You know it's the truth, Arthur. I only want Carol to know what she would be getting into." He gave her another of his comprehensive looks, just personal enough to make her pulse quicken. "She's a hothouse flower, Arthur, exotic and fragile, with that pale skin and delicate bone structure."

For a moment Carol eyed Simon balefully. She had never considered herself either exotic or fragile, but of course, to a man at least six feet two and muscularly built, she must appear frail.

"Appearances can be very deceiving, Simon," she said pointedly, unconscious of her use of his first name. "You obviously don't know me at all!"

"Only what I see for myself and read in the papers. Carol Durand, much-photographed granddaughter of old Carlton Durand. Heiress to the Durand Woolen Mills. Debutante of the season ten years ago. And a very sexy lady! But why don't you tell me more?" he invited. "I find myself with an overpowering ambition to know you very well!"

"Well, it's a shame that your ambitions don't have a hope of being realized!" she gasped, aware of the sudden flare of sexual antagonism between them. The realization shocked her. Simon was totally unlike any man she had been attracted to in the past.

"I'm a very determined man, Carol, not one to give up hope. That's something *you* need to know about *me!*"

He spoke with authority, as though their futures were somehow linked inevitably, and the warm intensity of his gaze sent a tingle up her spine.

"I'm not interested!" she protested breathlessly and not entirely truthfully.

"You see, Arthur?" Simon said with satisfaction. "Even Carol thinks it would be better if she didn't take Katie's case."

"I didn't say that!" Carol objected, rattled by the man's sudden shift.

"Then you'll take the case?" Arthur said quickly.

"I—I didn't say that either!"

Simon's lips twitched with amusement at her confusion. "I'd say the lady doesn't know *what* she wants."

Arthur jumped quickly into the tense silence that followed this gibe. "Look, Carol, I told you that you didn't have to decide today."

"Leave her alone, Arthur. Maine in winter would be a foreign habitat. A beautiful butterfly would get her wings frostbitten."

Carol took these as fighting words. "Most butterflies," she said firmly, "are blessed with a spirit of adventure, Mr. Forbes—" She bit back the remainder of her caustic retort as she was struck with a sudden unpalatable thought. "We . . . er, we wouldn't be *alone* on the island, would we?"

"An intriguing prospect," Simon said provocatively, with a swift perusal of her slender body that brought unwanted color into her cheeks. "And under other circumstances I would welcome the idea. But actually, no. I have help."

Carol was feeling more and more confused by Simon's attitude. He seemed to be beckoning her with one hand and rejecting her with the other. Wearily she rubbed the back of her neck. Emotional exhaustion and a sleepless night after her run-in with Rick had taken a lot out of her.

Professionally she was interested in Katie's case, but the thought of living in Simon's house, of having to see him day in and day out, was daunting. A few minutes in his company, and she was already undone. She had never met another man quite like him—disturbingly attractive, cultured and worldly in his own way, oozing sensual potency, but forthright to a fault.

Was that why Arthur had taken her to view his work the night before? To let her see the sensitivity that lay beneath the man's brusque candor? Simon Forbes, the artist.

How had she described his work? Like lightning. Exciting, stimulating, but also threatening. He himself was all that and more. He made no attempt to please her, did nothing to charm her, but still she knew that he was interested in her—as a woman, not as a therapist for his daughter!

"I—I really think," she stammered awkwardly, "that it might be better if Barb were to go and I stayed here, Arthur."

"Very wise, Carol," Simon said solemnly.

"Afraid?" Arthur asked dryly—coming, Carol thought with chagrin, much too close to the truth.

"Not at all, Arthur," she lied, unable to meet his too-knowing eyes. "I just think that Barb's nice ordinary middle-class background might suit Mr. Forbes better. I'm sure no one has ever called her a hothouse flower!"

"Sorry if that rankled." Simon grinned. "In the proper circumstances I'm *very* partial to the exotic. Have dinner with me tonight and I'll explain. Hmmm?"

"I'm not interested!" she repeated with less than the truth.

"Afraid, Carol?" he asked, mimicking Arthur's amused tone.

"Not at all! Just choosy!" she tossed off flippantly.

"Liar!"

"Children, children!" Arthur intervened, at his most avuncular. "Can we get back to the issue at hand? Katie is our major concern, remember? Carol, I don't want you to give me an answer now. Take the weekend to think it over."

"Carol obviously doesn't want to—" Simon began.

"Oh, do be quiet for a moment, Simon! Stop baiting Carol."

Arthur's comment brought her up short. Was the man deliberately baiting her? Why? Pride forced her to voice the question. "Why don't you want me, Mr. Forbes?"

"There's wanting and then there's wanting," he drawled, his voice heavy with innuendo.

Carol's lips tightened, but this time she refused to rise to the bait. "You're quick, Simon, but this time it won't work. Just what do you have against my working with Katie?"

The direct approach succeeded. Simon frowned and shot a sideways glance at Arthur. The doctor quickly took the hint. "Uh, why don't I just leave you two alone for a few minutes to sort this out between you? Call me when you're ready." Before Carol could protest he had whisked himself out the door.

"Okay," she sighed in resignation. "Let's have it."

Reluctantly he began. "Carol, I may be a layman where psychology is concerned, but I've done a good deal of reading up on Katie's ailment —enough to know that you don't treat a child like her in isolation. Whatever happened to her involved myself, my wife, my entire household."

"So?" she prompted when he stopped.

"So you would come into my life with the intention of poking and prying into my most intimate affairs, probing *my* life and mind as much as Katie's."

"But I'm a doctor, Simon!"

"If you took Katie's case," he continued harshly, ignoring her interruption, "you would have to turn me inside out, looking for weaknesses, inconsistencies, repressions, dark shadows that I would rather keep hidden. You would end up knowing more about me than I know about myself—or am willing to admit. How is a man supposed to feel about that kind of invasion of his privacy? Hmmm? And by a *woman*—a woman he would like to do his best to impress! How would *you* like the idea of going to bed with your own gynecologist? Not an exact analogy, but close enough!"

"There's no question of our—!" Carol gasped.

"—going to bed together? Isn't there? You're a very, very beautiful woman, Carol, and sexy as hell. I wanted to make love to you the first minute I laid eyes on you."

"Well, what if I'm not interested?" she said faintly, her heart racing at the look in his eyes.

He shrugged. "That's your choice. It doesn't stop me from feeling the way I do about you. Can you understand why I don't want you in my home as Katie's doctor?"

Slowly Carol digested this. Yes, it did make sense to her, and she could understand his conflicting emotions. What he said about the nature of her work was true. A doctor did not treat a patient like Katie in isolation. To get to the heart of the child's problem, Carol would have to find out every relevant piece of information about her family, her extended family, her friends—every person she had been in close contact with at the critical time. Right now Carol was in perfect agreement with Simon Forbes. She wasn't sure she wanted to know that much about him—as a man! After the debacle with Rick, she was feeling too bruised, too vulnerable.

Carol's silent contemplation had obviously begun to etch itself on Simon's nerves. "Well?" he asked curtly.

In answer Carol turned and opened the door to Arthur's office. "Arthur?"

He arrived so promptly that she knew he had been hovering just outside.

"Arthur," she began, "I don't think—"

"Please, Carol," the psychiatrist stopped her. "I don't want you to give me an answer now. Take the weekend to think it over. I'll talk to you Monday."

"But—"

"Leave us now, if you would, please. I want to talk a little sense into Simon."

She couldn't ignore such an obvious dismissal. "Very well." The smile she turned on Simon was ironic. "I must say, *Mr. Forbes,* that meeting you has been an experience!"

"I would class it more in the nature of an event, *Dr. Durand,*" he said slowly, returning her smile in kind.

"One of a kind, let's hope!" she exclaimed, her heart doing flip-flops at the impact of that smile.

"Carol!"

"All right, Arthur. I'm going." As she left, she had the distinct impression that Simon was laughing at her.

Two hours later Carol pulled her white Mercedes into the small drive that circled up to the back steps of the town house. Hawkins, the butler, had obviously been watching for her and had the door open before she could take out her key.

"Good afternoon, Miss Carol," he greeted her formally, but with the warmth of an old friend and valued member of the household. "Mrs. Durand is waiting for you in the drawing room and would like to see you before you change for dinner. Oh, and I put the flowers from Mr. Sanders in the front hallway."

Carol paused in the act of taking off her driving gloves, and then turned slowly to allow Hawkins to help her off with her coat.

"Did he have the flowers sent or bring them himself?" she asked casually.

"Oh, he came himself, Miss Carol, just about an hour ago."

"I take it he didn't stay."

"Well, no, miss. He spent some time with Mrs. Durand and then left. Should she have detained him?"

"No!" she said sharply, and then, more quietly, "No, but Hawkins, if he should come again, I don't wish to see him, and would you please inform the staff that I won't be taking any calls from him—ever!"

This statement shook the elderly butler out of his habitual calm. "Ever, miss?"

"That's right!"

"Oh, dear!"

He was looking very disturbed. "Is something the matter?" she asked, more sharply than she had intended.

"I really can't say, Miss Carol, but I think it would be well if you talked with your aunt immediately."

"I'll just do that." Carol walked briskly down

the broad hallway that bisected the house from front to back. At the door to the drawing room she could not help but notice the huge bouquet of pink and white long-stemmed roses that held the place of honor on the antique chest. The gilt mirror behind reflected what must have been ten dozen blooms, but Carol took no pleasure in the sight.

There was one good thing about her encounter with Simon Forbes, she concluded wryly. The man had pushed all thoughts of Rick Sanders from her mind! And now she resented Rick's intrusion once again in the form of an expensive apology. A useless apology, she thought darkly as pain and anger returned. Picking up the card that Hawkins had placed beside the vase, she tore it once across, then tossed it into the wastebasket.

Her aunt Cora was perched elegantly on the edge of a brocade chair when she entered the drawing room, obviously waiting expectantly for Carol's arrival.

"There you are, my dear!" the older woman said in her deep Bostonian tones. "You just missed Rick, poor man! He brought you a lovely bouquet of flowers. Such a charming, thoughtful person. So well mannered, so well connected!" she added with satisfaction.

"Cora," Carol interjected quickly, "I'm not going to be seeing Rick Sanders anymore."

Cora Durand's mouth tightened perceptibly and she raised her beautifully coiffed gray head to a height of regal command that would have made a younger Carol quail. "Rick told me that you two young people had had a little lovers' quarrel," she said with distaste. "I know you have a lamentable tendency to lose your temper now and then, but Carol, you know that Rick loves you dearly, and if you apologize I'm sure he is more than willing to forgive you—"

"Cora!"

Her aunt stiffened at the sharp note in her niece's voice. "Yes?"

"Cora, I am not going to be seeing Rick Sanders again," she repeated, more firmly this time.

"But of course you are!" The older woman checked the watch pinned to the bodice of her mauve lace dress. "In fact, you will be seeing him again in just about one hour. I invited him to dinner tonight—"

"You've invited him to dinner!" Carol snapped, riding ruthlessly over the end of her aunt's sentence.

"Why, yes. The poor man was quite distraught. Such nonsense! I will say this for you, my dear. You may lose your temper now and then, but you're never one to hold grudges—"

"I don't want to see him!" Carol said firmly, breaking into what threatened to be a lengthy monologue on her weaknesses and virtues.

"Now, don't be absurd, Carol. Of course you want to see Rick. Why, he told me only this afternoon that he's just waiting for you to set the wedding date. Such a wonderful match for you! I've said often that it's well past time you settled down and started your family. You know I've never approved of your having a career. . . ."

Carol gave up the futile attempt to stop her

aunt's favorite lecture. She was fond of Cora in spite of the woman's overbearing manner and constant attempts to interfere in her personal affairs.

The headache that had been threatening burst into full bloom as Cora began to wax eloquent. Tuning out her aunt's voice, Carol concentrated on the problem at hand. She had to get out of the house before Rick arrived. He had wounded something deep inside her with his condemnation of her, and she never, never wanted to see him again! He had managed to wangle a dinner invitation out of Cora, but Carol had no intention of being there.

Oh, but she was so exhausted, both emotionally and physically, just as Arthur had said. Arthur!

Give yourself a change of scene . . . a breathing space.

Was that the answer? Escape? Escape, not just from this evening's encounter with Rick, but for long enough for Rick to turn his attention to someone else?

Suddenly a lonely, isolated island seemed like a godsend. Any trepidation she felt about Simon Forbes paled to insignificance beside the thought of being forced to see Rick, being constantly under the curious eyes of their friends and acquaintances. He would be impossible to avoid, especially with her aunt on his side.

She shuddered at the thought of the inevitable gossip that would be bound to greet their breaking up. She couldn't bear it, not so soon after the affair with Brian.

"—I'm sure you agree, Carol. Don't you?"

Carol focused on Cora's bright, expectant face. At that moment she couldn't imagine agreeing with anything her aunt had to say. "Cora," she said firmly, "I've got to go and change now. I'm having dinner with Arthur tonight."

"What?"

For once, she thought with wry amusement, she had startled her aunt into silence. "I said, I'm having dinner with Arthur tonight."

"But my dear, you can't! What about Rick?"

"Just explain to him that I had a previous engagement. He'll understand." She added to herself, He'd better understand!

She didn't wait around to hear any more. If Rick was expected in less than an hour, she had no time to waste. It took her only ten minutes to change out of her slacks and blazer and into a cocktail dress. She had to keep up the fiction of an engagement, if only to stem the tide of her aunt's recriminations.

Fortunately Hawkins hadn't had time to send one of the boys out to garage the car and it stood where she had left it in the drive.

"Please, Carol!" Cora twittered fretfully as Carol grabbed the keys from the hook on the wall. "What am I going to tell Rick?"

"I'm sure you'll think of something. I've never known you at a loss for words," she returned with an irony she knew would escape her aunt.

"But—!"

Carol didn't wait to hear the rest.

Twenty minutes later she pulled up in front of the modest Cape Cod home in Cambridge where

Arthur had lived for many years. His elderly housekeeper welcomed her with a smile.

"The doctor is in his study, Miss Durand. Go right on back."

Carol found Arthur nodding off in his leather easy chair in front of a roaring fire, and she sat down quietly opposite him.

"Arthur," she said softly.

"Hmmm? Hmmm! Carol! Didn't hear you come in!" Sleep was instantly banished as he took in her high color and the nervous twitch of the muscle at the side of her mouth.

"I'm sorry to disturb you at home, Arthur, but I wanted to talk to you."

"Something that couldn't wait?"

"Yes."

"You've made a decision about the Forbes child," he said.

"That's right. I'll take her case."

Chapter Three

The week that ensued was a severe trial of Carol's normally sunny disposition. Rick hounded and plagued her with daily deliveries of flowers, impassioned notes and continual phone calls. The flowers she gave to the servants, the notes she tore up unread and she refused to receive his calls. Cora never let an opportunity to champion Rick's cause go by. She alternately commanded and pleaded, until finally Carol threatened to move into a hotel. This cast her aunt into an offended silence that was almost as hard to bear as the recriminations had been. Only the knowledge that she was soon to escape sustained Carol through the week's ordeal.

When she finally informed Cora that she was leaving Boston for an indefinite stay in Maine, the woman took it as a personal affront.

"You're a heartless girl, Carol Durand," she snapped. "You will dwindle into a hardened, bitter old spinster and it serves you right! I simply do not understand how you can be so cruel to a wonderful, socially prominent man like Rick Sanders!"

Carol held her tongue. Through all the hullabaloo she had refused to discuss Rick with Cora, less, she admitted to herself, from a desire to protect Rick's image than because of the lowering suspicion that Cora would hold Carol responsible for their quarrel. She knew what her aunt would say. Carol had led him on, kept him dangling, provoked him. What was the poor man to do? Cora had been raised to know a woman's place— subservient to the dominant, superior male, knowledgeable in the kitchen and dutiful in the bedroom.

The only saving factor in the interminable week was that Carol had been spared another encounter with Simon Forbes and she was able to delude herself that she could cope with the man once he had reconciled himself to the fact that she had taken the case. Yes, she could handle Simon Forbes. All she had to do was treat the situation with her usual professional detachment.

With great relief Carol finally left Boston well behind her. She glanced down at the map on the seat beside her. Following Simon's letter of instructions, she had turned off the interstate at Brunswick and dropped down onto the coastal highway. Now she was nearly to Boothbay, as far into Maine as she had ever been. From Boothbay

it was a matter of a little over a hundred miles to
Bar Harbor on Mount Desert Island. With luck
she would be there by mid-afternoon. That would
give her a couple of hours before she was to meet
the boat for the last leg of her journey to Porcupine Island.

Happily she turned her attention to the rugged
Maine terrain. What wonderful country! Pine
forests interspersed with patches of cultivated
farmland dominated the landscape. The coastline
itself was comprised of gigantic rocks, with very
little beach. The surf pounded the shore, sending
the foaming spray into the air like a series of small
geysers.

In her mind's eye she had a sudden picture of
Simon Forbes as she had seen him last—rugged,
vital, a little overwhelming—and she couldn't
help but conclude that this wild landscape suited
his forceful personality far better than did the
refined urbanity of Boston.

It was later than Carol had anticipated when
she finally reached the outskirts of Bar Harbor.
The highway had been slower going than the
interstate and she hadn't been able to resist the
urge to stop and get a better look at a lighthouse
perched on a rocky promontory. With each new
mile between herself and Rick Sanders she felt a
wonderful sense of freedom, of expanding hori-
zons, of having escaped a suffocating trap. Yes,
she had made the right decision.

Resolutely she put Rick out of her mind. Bar
Harbor was an interesting enough town to deserve her total attention. A few of the huge

private estates still remained, but many had been converted into resort hotels. The summer months, she knew, brought hordes of tourists who were visiting Acadia National Park, and at a glance, tourism seemed to be the major industry of the island. Restaurants, motels and curio shops lined the main street, but there was still an appealing picturesqueness to the place.

Fortunately it didn't take long to find a hotel willing to house her car. While the park remained open all year, only the hardiest of tourists ventured to the island during the severe winter season. After a quick cup of coffee she arranged for help with her luggage and made her way down to the pier, only a minute or two ahead of the appointed time.

Would Simon Forbes himself be there to meet her? And if not, she wondered, how would she know whom to approach? She wished his instructions had been more explicit.

Simon was there, waiting by a sleek cabin cruiser, but it took her a moment to recognize him. Gone were the well-tailored city clothes. Instead he was dressed in faded jeans that hugged his long, muscular legs. A plaid wool jacket hung open over a navy blue T-shirt and a dark captain's hat was pulled down over his disordered hair. He stood with his feet apart, his hands on his narrow hips, his head thrown back as he savored the sting of the salt breeze. A faint stubble gave his face a swarthy appearance. In fact, there was very little about him that appeared civilized. He looked like a throwback to some pirate ancestor.

All he needed, Carol concluded, was an earring, a saber at his side and a skull and crossbones flying above the deck of his boat!

Her heart began to pound as she quickened her steps—but not from the pace. The sight of Simon Forbes stirred something fundamental in her that she hesitated to name. Antagonism played a large part, and yet she didn't dislike him. Actually, she had a great deal of healthy respect for him, both as an artist and as a man. She had reached this particular conclusion after one nerve-racking day of dodging Rick. Polite society might smile on Rick's charm, sophistication and polished manner, but she knew that they masked a very unpleasant character. She might find Simon's frankness disconcerting, but at least he was honest.

Cool and professional, she counseled herself as she approached him. Just play it cool and professional.

His eyes were following her progress down the length of the pier and as she drew near she read a faintly hostile yet openly admiring gleam there. Despite the fact that she had dressed warmly in a chunky tweed pantsuit and a heavy turtlenecked sweater, Simon managed to make her feel intensely feminine, and her heart jumped erratically in response.

"Good afternoon, Mr. Forbes," she said as she joined him, hoping he would put her breathlessness down to exertion. "I hope I haven't kept you waiting."

"Too little, too late, Carol," he said dryly.

"We've gone long past impersonal formality, I'm afraid."

Truth be told, Carol was beginning to fear the same, but it seemed the best course for both of them. "I—I think it would be better to try."

"Suit yourself." He shrugged. "But I'm not much into game playing myself. Where's your luggage?" He looked suddenly hopeful, as though she had perhaps changed her mind about staying on the island.

"A man from the hotel is bringing it down. In fact, here he is now."

"This lady going with you, Simon?" the elderly handyman puffed, his eyes bright with interest, his Yankee accent pronounced. "She didn't tell me who she was meeting."

"Miss Durand is a . . . teacher for my daughter," Simon returned casually, but Carol noted the omission of her title and felt the wall of reserve that had suddenly been erected.

"Yeah? Heard you brought the poor little tyke back with you." His eyes swept over Carol in a quick, studied glance. "Teacher, eh? That mean Katie's going to stay with you for a while?"

"Yes."

"How's she doing? She talkin' yet?" The man was either dense or chose to ignore the repressive note in Simon's replies.

"She's fine, thank you, Almo."

"Mrs. Penrod coming to stay, too?" Almo persisted curiously.

Who was Mrs. Penrod? Carol wondered. Obviously not someone Simon chose to discuss.

His mouth firmed into a hard line. "No," he replied curtly.

"Can't say I blame her," the man continued. "Mighty lonely out there this time of year." His eyes skimmed over Carol's trim form. "Mighty lonely. Glad *you've* got some company."

Simon frowned darkly and ended further conversation by picking up Carol's suitcases and dumping them over the side of the boat.

"Let's be off, Miss Durand." The hotel man's insinuations had been far from subtle and Simon had apparently decided that impersonal formality was not so pointless after all. He held out a peremptory hand to assist her into the boat. "Here!"

At least he didn't plan on dumping her in as unceremoniously as the luggage! She shivered, and not from the cold. This was a side of Simon she had not seen before. His displeasure was very chilling. There was nothing chilling, however, about the warmth of his hand as she took it. As his fingers tightened she remembered the strength of those artist's hands.

"Want I should cast off for you?" the man asked helpfully, apparently undaunted by Simon's manner.

"Thanks, Almo. I'd appreciate it."

Spurning the steps, Simon jumped into the craft with the grace and ease of long experience, disappeared into the cabin and slammed the door closed after him. A moment later the powerful twin engines roared into life. Carol stood hesitantly on the rear deck, uncertain what to do next. The matter of where to sit was quickly settled as Simon set the boat in motion with a sudden burst of speed that propelled her awkwardly onto the rear bench.

"Well!" she gasped indignantly, clutching her purse and tote bag to her side as the boat sped out of the protected bay and into the deep green waters of the Atlantic. Not by so much as a glance did Simon acknowledge the presence of his passenger.

Well, she amended the thought. This was what she had wanted—wasn't it? She had wanted Simon to forget about her as a woman and accept her as a trained specialist for Katie. Still, an unwelcome feminine pique at the speed with which he had made the adjustment brought color to her cheeks. She had old Almo to thank for that, she supposed. He had brought the potential difficulties of the situation home.

Forget Simon Forbes, she told herself. Relax. Enjoy the ride.

Land was quickly receding into the distance and becoming nothing but a blur on the horizon. All around them was sea, dotted occasionally with a returning fishing trawler. The sun was sinking lower and lower, spotting the tops of the waves with golden highlights.

Twenty minutes out of Bar Harbor Carol had her first glimpse of Porcupine Island—a small dark speck in a vast ocean. As they drew nearer she saw that much of the darkness was caused by the giant white pine trees that dominated the island and created the impression of spiny quills.

From her vantage point she noted that the island was wedge shaped, sloping up gently from sea level on one side, but with cliffs rising a hundred feet or more on the other. As yet there was no sign of a house or any other indication of habitation. In fact, the coastline appeared very formidable and virtually unnegotiable.

They were perhaps a mile away when the boat veered to the left to approach the island from the far side and Carol saw where Simon was heading. A small bay, almost totally protected by surrounding rocks, formed a natural harbor. The channel opening to the bay at first appeared so narrow that she wondered how even this small craft could pass through. But as Simon slowed the engines and headed toward the opening she realized that the inlet was actually wider than she had suspected, perhaps thirty feet. Even so, the currents were strong and she knew that he had to exercise considerable skill to bring them through safely and dock the boat at the small pier.

As Simon cut the engines and joined her on deck Carol caught her first glimpse of life. A face appeared in the doorway of the boat house and a huge lumbering body quickly followed. The bay was in shadow, but she could still catch the broad grin that split the man's homely face.

"You're back in good time, Simon. I thought you were going to have to come in in the dark."

"Miss Durand was right on time, Sam."

"She sure is a pretty little thing, isn't she?" Sam replied, eyeing Carol with open appreciation. "Pretty hair. Natural, too. You can tell."

Simon's eyes focused on Carol's windblown hair. "I've noticed," he said curtly.

"Real pretty!" There was a reverence in Sam's tone that made it impossible for Carol to take offense and she found herself smiling at his almost childlike awe.

"Sam will bring up your luggage after he takes care of the boat," Simon said tersely, handing her onto the dock and swinging up beside her. "Let's go."

"Let's go where?" she asked, stung by his abruptness as he strode off down the pier, leaving her to follow in his wake.

"Home, of course," he called without stopping.

She had asked for formality, not surliness! she thought in exasperation, half running to keep up with his long measured strides as he headed toward a flight of wooden steps.

"Well, considering the fact that there's no house in sight, you might forgive me for asking!" she called to his retreating back. At over six feet, he eclipsed her by a full head, and most of his height, she concluded bitterly, was in his legs. "Oh, for heaven's sake, will you slow down?"

He turned and stopped so abruptly that she almost bashed into him and for an instant she was struck with the delightful thought that, had she kept going, she might have pushed him into the bay. Wishful thinking, she concluded gloomily as her arm came into contact with his broad chest. He was built like a brick wall. Her irritation rose as he backed away from her as though he had been stung.

"You've got a mighty smart mouth for a doctor," he said curtly.

"Just inspired by my company," she retorted.

"As a psychologist you ought to know better than to play with fire!" he snapped, something other than hostility bringing a bright flare into his eyes. "I told Arthur this was going to be impossible," he muttered. "Why couldn't you have stayed in Boston where you belong?"

Carol was beginning to wonder the same thing, and her temper wasn't improved by the knowledge that she herself was responsible for being here. If she had declined to come Arthur wouldn't have forced her. . . . Suddenly she frowned. But on the other hand, Simon could have refused to have her and demanded another therapist.

"Why did you agree to have me take the case, if that's the way you feel about me?" she asked defensively.

"You know very well why! Arthur made it a condition of my gaining custody of Katie. I had no choice. You did!"

"Simon, I had no idea! He never told me!"

He looked at her for a hard moment, read the truth in her candid brown eyes and shrugged. "So, let's get on with it. Do you want me to go first and lead the way, or would you prefer that I follow and catch you when you fall, city girl?"

This was deliberate provocation, but for once Carol didn't rise to the bait.

"Please, Simon, could we call a temporary truce? I don't know about you, but I've had a long, hard day. I was up before daylight to finish packing. I've driven a couple of hundred miles and you've hardly had a kind word to say to me since the moment I arrived! I'm not asking for sympathy, but if you'd show a little compassion and wait to renew hostilities until I'm back in condition, I'd consider it very sporting of you."

A strong breeze had come up over the water and not even Carol's tweed jacket could keep out the chill. She shivered, and she saw Simon's expression soften.

"I'm sorry, Carol. You have so much spirit that sometimes I forget you're just a little slip of a thing. The house is only about a quarter of a mile away through the trees and once we're up the steps the trail is only moderately steep. Ada, my housekeeper, will be waiting with hot coffee and then you can have an hour to rest before dinner."

She appreciated his capitulation and smiled in relief. "Hot coffee sounds wonderful! Why don't you lead on?"

In answer he put out his hand to her and its strength and warmth brought an immediate security. She couldn't help but compare it with Rick's. Rick's fingernails were always kept beautifully manicured and had never known what it was to be encrusted with clay. Any calluses he had developed had come from a strenuous tennis tournament at the club or a polo match. His hands had never known the effects of having to work for a living, and their softness was as deliberately cultivated as the strength and toughness of Simon's.

Unconsciously, she tightened her fingers and Simon returned the pressure. "Let's go."

The steps were easier to negotiate than they had appeared. The pitch was steep, but the treads were wide. Not until they neared the top did she stumble, and then only because Simon had increased his speed and the shadow of the trees had left the last three steps in total darkness.

Simon felt her start to fall. His grip on her hand tightened and instinctively he put out his other arm to steady her. Neatly his hand slipped around her slim waist and he held her against his side until she could regain her footing. She had never been this close to him before. Her senses were assaulted by his smell—the aroma of tobacco, sweat and salt from the sea. It was a healthy male smell, totally unlike Rick's expensive cologne. Her heart began to beat faster as she felt the intimacy of the moment in these primitive surroundings.

"All right?" Simon asked when she didn't move. The muscles in his arm tightened, bringing her even closer, and she felt the pounding of a heart—his or hers? His hard strength left her breathless. Urgently she drew in a sharp breath and her breasts rose hard against his side.

"Are you all right?" he repeated.

"I—I'm fine," she stuttered, trying to regain her composure. His hold loosened and she moved quickly away from his disturbing nearness.

The path through the trees was broad enough to accommodate them both. Simon kept her hand in his and even though the grip was light, she still felt its potency.

Halfway along the path she had her first

glimpse of the house—her home for the next weeks. Both the interior and exterior lights had been turned on, presumably to help guide their way. Her first impression was of a medieval fortress perched on the top of the rocks. Stone parapets and towers of granite shone white through the tops of the trees. It was an extraordinary house, huge, rugged, daunting—perfectly suited to its master!

"Something wrong?" he asked as her footsteps slowed.

"N-nothing!" she gulped. "Is—is that the house up ahead?"

"An astute deduction."

"You said you lived primitively!" she challenged him. "That—that's a castle!"

"Did you expect a wooden shack?"

"You were just trying to frighten me!" she exclaimed. "I should have remembered that ogres —even modern ones—live in castles!"

"So I'm an ogre, am I?" His lips twitched in amusement at her indignation. "And naturally you've cast yourself as a captive princess. Just who do you have in mind for Prince Charming? Not that blond Adonis I saw you with at the gallery last week, I hope. I'm not sure he'd be up to scaling any walls."

Carol had begun to enjoy the quick banter—up to the point where Simon alluded to Rick. At that she stiffened. The thought of Rick somehow tracking her down was appalling. The primary reason she had allowed herself to become involved with Simon Forbes and his daughter had been the assurance she felt that Rick could never find her here!

"Now what did I say, I wonder?" Simon mused thoughtfully. "I struck a nerve, apparently."

His perception disconcerted her, though heaven knew she ought to be getting used to it by now.

"Oh, let's get inside," she snapped. "I'm cold!"

"And mighty touchy, too, it seems. What happened? Did you and the boyfriend have a fight?" he asked, his eyes alight with interest.

"It's none of your business."

"Oh, no? When you took this case you chose to make my personal life your business. The way I see it, I have some rights, too. *I've* chosen to make everything about you my business as well!"

"What if I don't choose to let you?"

"You will. You're stuck here now, and there's no going back. I've got the courts, Katie's grandmother, even Arthur, breathing down my neck. I can't send you away just because having you here happens to be hard on my ego. I'll save my pride some way."

He was looking down into her face with such an intensity that she felt a tingle along her spine like a jolt of electricity and she caught her breath.

"But I'm a doctor!" she reminded him weakly.

Her words only brought a derisive glint into his eyes, and before she could retreat he caught her hard against him, one arm pinned along her body, the other trapped against his chest.

"You don't *look* like a doctor," he said huskily, his voice deep with suppressed desire. "You don't *feel* like a doctor." His hold tightened. "Shall we see if you *act* like a doctor? Why don't you show me how you maintain your professional distance, how you stay calm and rational and detached?"

She didn't realize his intention until she felt his fingers trail down her cheek and come to rest on her chin. By then she was beyond stopping him as he tilted her head back against his shoulder. She only had time to murmur one halfhearted protest before his lips found hers. He had caught her mouth parted and he took full advantage of her vulnerability to explore and savor its sweetness.

Carol had been kissed many times before— with warmth, hunger and passion—but nothing in her experience equaled the sheer mastery of Simon's embrace. He demanded nothing but allowed the gentle, tender probing of his lips and tongue to arouse their own irresistible response.

Weakly she clung to him, vaguely troubled that she was putting up no resistance, futile though it would have been. Her strength was puny compared with Simon's. As her arms slipped around his back of their own volition she was forced to admit that she didn't want to resist him. At a later time she would analyze why, but for now she just wanted to enjoy the exquisite pleasure of his kiss, the excitement of his hard, firm body pressed against hers. Her feet were barely touching the ground, so tightly did he hold her, and she experienced the heady sensation of being totally absorbed into the embrace.

Gradually he lowered her feet to the path and raised his head, only to bury it against her hair, fanning the soft skin of her ear with his breath. For a moment Carol was too profoundly stirred by his kiss to say anything and Simon pulled back to look down into her face. She was grateful that the encroaching darkness made it impossible for him to read her reactions.

"Well?" Simon prompted. "Who did you kiss, Carol? The man or the client?"

"I—I think the situation is too precarious to joke about, Simon," she replied shakily.

"Who's joking? I wanted to show you that you're not exactly a disinterested observer in this whole thing. Here I am, torn between my own personal desires and my duty to my child."

"With me caught right in the middle! Not a very comfortable position to be in!"

"I warned you that your situation wouldn't be comfortable here, if you'll remember. I did my best to discourage you."

"You warned me about the isolation, about the climate, about the inconveniences, Simon Forbes. What you didn't warn me about was *you!*"

"You're the psychologist," he drawled.

"Oh, let's go!" she cried, her thoughts in turmoil, her nerves still unstrung by Simon's embrace. "The sooner I get to work with Katie, the better it's going to be for all of us!"

On closer inspection the house was no less intimidating than it had appeared from a distance. Huge studded pine doors guarded the entrance and the granite walls themselves must have been two feet thick. Before Simon could touch the latch the double doors were flung wide and a middle-aged woman stood framed dramatically in the doorway, her purple caftan fluttering in the breeze.

"Hello, Ada," Simon said warmly.

"Simon!" The woman's voice was deep and throaty and confirmed Carol's first impression that this woman belonged on a stage. "Darling, I was just ready to send Arnold out looking for you! Sam radioed from the boathouse half an hour ago to say you had arrived!" Her smiling eyes moved from Simon to Carol, who was standing behind him. "And this must be Dr. Durand. Welcome, my dear. Welcome to Forbes Castle."

She stood aside and gestured them in to the huge entrance hall. The room rose straight up two stories to where an encircling balcony loomed overhead in darkness. The light from the gigantic brass chandelier did little to dispel the gloom and shadows that lurked in every corner.

"Well, what do you think, Carol?" Simon asked, amusement in his voice.

For a moment Carol was too enthralled to speak. Then, as she looked up into Simon's face, she was struck by the notion that he was overwhelming enough in normal surroundings, but in his own castle he took on the proportions not of an ogre but of a conquering warrior!

"Coffee will be getting cold." Ada broke in on Carol's reveries.

What an extraordinary house! Carol concluded as she hurried to follow Simon across the flagstone hall, past the long flight of stone steps rising to the upper floor and through an arched doorway in the far wall to the room beyond. This small salon was homey in appearance, especially in comparison with the other rooms she had glimpsed. Carol's spirits lifted at the sight of the roaring fire. The only furniture in the entry hall had been carved wooden benches and high-backed wooden chairs, but this room had been furnished for comfort rather than with an austere simplicity.

An upholstered couch flanked by two leather easy chairs created a conversation area in front of the fireplace and a white fur rug covered the parquet floor. Various lamps and tables were placed in convenient locations and a huge arrangement of pinecones and berries added a living warmth to the room.

She and Simon had hardly seated themselves when a shy, thin girl of perhaps nineteen or twenty arrived with the tea cart. She ducked her face behind lank brown hair as she caught Carol's eye, but blushed with pleasure when Simon smiled at her warmly. "Thank you, Amy."

After the girl had arranged the coffee on the table in front of them with meticulous care and hurried out, Carol turned to Simon. The sight that met her eyes caused a momentary pang in the region of her heart. He lay with his head resting against the high back of the chair, his eyes closed, the lines of strain around his mouth pronounced.

"Simon," she said hesitantly, "do you want to talk about Katie now, or would you rather wait until later?"

"No, let's get the preliminaries over with. What do you want to know first?"

Carol took the time to pour them each a cup of coffee and marshal her thoughts. "Cream or sugar?" she asked absently.

"If that's all you want to know," Simon replied wryly, "we'll get along just fine."

"Don't get your hopes up." She sighed. "I'm really having to start from scratch. Arthur's records show nothing but Katie's medical tests and personal history. Therapy was never really started."

"Madge," he said tersely. "Angela's mother. The decision was left up to her."

The bitterness in his voice took Carol by surprise, and she filed it away for future reference. His mother-in-law would have to wait. Right now there was a more important piece of information she needed. How had Angela Forbes died? The file had indicated nothing but a freak accident. What kind of accident, and where?

Carol pushed personal considerations aside and allowed her professional concerns to dominate her thoughts. Katie's welfare came first, which meant she had to deal with Simon the client, not Simon the man.

She studied him for a moment, looking beyond his attractiveness. What was he thinking? His head was back, his face turned toward the fire, but she knew he wasn't seeing the leaping flames. A bleakness had settled over his expression, making him look older than his years. He had taken off his hat when he entered the house, and now, in the flickering light of the fire, she caught the smatterings of gray in his dark hair, in the short sideburns and at his temples. He appeared calm and relaxed, but Carol saw the signs of tension. His fingers gripped the arms of the chair, the knuckles so white that they threw the large protruding blue veins along the backs of his hands into strong contrast.

For all his openness, Carol knew that he was a complex man with depths to his personality she could only guess at. His artwork told her that. Such expressive hands, she mused idly. So capable of giving expression to lifeless matter. Yes, a very complex man—outwardly so strong, so seemingly invulnerable, but inwardly . . . inwardly, what? His work demonstrated a sensitivity, an understanding of human nature and, yes, even a tenderness, that had to be an inherent part of his personality.

"Simon," she said abruptly, "I'm sorry that Arthur forced me on you, sorry if I've made things difficult—"

"The situation with Katie would be difficult under the best of circumstances, Carol," he admitted frankly. "I told you, it's too late for regrets. Too late for a lot of things," he murmured enigmatically, and a shuttered look came over his eyes, making it impossible for her to read their expression.

"I'm going to do my best with Katie, you know that, don't you? But you already understand that I need your cooperation. Besides what you refer to as the poking and prying, you've got to help me understand her. It's much more difficult working with a child who doesn't speak. She's able to keep a lot more bottled up inside herself. She doesn't give anything away easily. She won't blurt out something in anger or frustration. All I can do is look for clues in the things she does and the way she reacts."

"What do you do? How do you work with her?" His questions were filled with interest and Carol took hope. No matter what his personal feelings might be, in her work with Katie she could be sure of his support.

"First I have to win her confidence, and then I have to find ways to make her respond to her surroundings and to me."

"So, what do you want to know?"

Carol hesitated. They were both very tired, but the sooner she had answers to the more difficult questions, the sooner she would know how best to proceed.

"Simon," she said slowly, "how exactly did Katie's mother die?"

"Arthur didn't tell you?" he asked bleakly.

"No, he only said she had been killed in an accident. I'm—I'm sorry to have to ask. I know it must still be very painful for you to talk about."

"A year can heal a lot of wounds," he said cryptically, and Carol wasn't entirely sure he was speaking only of his wife's death.

"So, did it happen near here?" she prompted.

"Not near here. Here."

"You mean, in the house?"

"Yes. She was coming down the stairs in the front hall. She tripped. Her neck was broken."

He spoke so impersonally, so dispassionately, that it was hard to believe he was speaking of his wife. "It—it must have come as a terrible shock to you," she said inadequately.

"A shock, yes."

"She must have been quite young."

"Twenty-six. We had been married eight years."

"How—how horrible for you!"

His eyes on hers were a bright, icy blue. "If you're asking if I grieved for her, the answer is no. I'm not telling you anything that wasn't general knowledge. We hadn't been . . . living together for several years before she died. There are some people who will even tell you that I helped her on her way down the stairs." His voice was hard and bitter.

She studied his face, frozen now into an impassive mask. When she finally spoke, it was with an inner conviction she couldn't account for rationally.

"But you didn't, did you?" she asked softly, thoughtfully, confidently. Calmly she withstood his hard scrutiny of her face. What he read there seemed to reassure him and she watched the tension drain from him.

"No, no, I didn't," he said tersely. "But you might want to ask Katie about it sometime in the future and watch how she reacts. You see, I think she believes I did."

Chapter Four

*Y*ou win again, Katie." Carol smiled as Katie made her final move. "Maybe checkers just isn't my game." The smile that Katie gave her was a pathetic thing of its kind, but it did allow the dimple in her cheek to peep out for just a moment.

She was a lovely child, Carol thought fondly. Her face was triangular and still much too thin, but her eyes were the same deep blue as her father's and her dark brown hair had the same copper highlights. She would be tall, too, like her father, Carol mused, and slim hipped.

Stop it! she chided herself as a picture of Simon rose in her mind's eye. She had found herself thinking about him much too often in the past week. Goodness knew she had seen little enough of him! Since that first evening, when he had dropped the bombshell about his wife's death, she hadn't had an opportunity to talk with him alone again. Whether he was purposely avoiding her or his work took him away she didn't know. But except for dinner, presided over by a loquacious Ada, or an occasional chance meeting in the hall, he kept to himself.

A tug on her skirt brought her attention back to her small patient. Katie had neatly put the game away and now had her head cocked as though to say: what now?

Carol glanced at her watch. Their hour was nearly up. "Let's play one more game and then it will be time for you to go downstairs to Amy for your snack. Watch what I do and follow me."

She stood up and smoothed her sweater down over the jeans she habitually wore when she played with Katie.

"I clap my hands—one, two, three," she began reciting, suiting the action to the words. "I tap my foot—very quietly. . . ."

As she watched the child mimic her actions she was delighted with the progress Katie had made during their sessions together. The first three days had been very difficult, as she had known they would be. For two days Carol had kept the maid, Amy, in the playroom with them, asking that the girl join with her in the various games and exercises she tried. Katie had stubbornly refused to participate at first.

Then, on the third day, they had constructed an elaborate castle with doors and windows and Katie had been tempted into joining them when it came time to put on the final turrets—a small beginning, but a major breakthrough. With only minor setbacks Carol had progressed steadily for the next four days. She had increased the play sessions from half an hour to an hour a time, and beginning the next day, she would increase them to two hours.

She wished Simon would show more interest, she thought, puzzled by his absence from the playroom. She couldn't believe that he didn't care about Katie's progress.

". . . down low—as far as I can go.
Then stretch up high and touch the
    sky . . ."

Katie's tongue was tucked into the corner of her mouth as she worked diligently to follow Carol.

Perhaps Simon believed she would prefer not to have his distracting presence in the room while she was working with Katie. Maybe that was what kept him away. Or did his obvious dislike of the mother extend to the child? she wondered, troubled.

"And sink right down, clear to the ground—" She stopped abruptly as Katie failed to follow her down to a sitting position on the floor. "What is it, Katie? What's the matter?"

The child appeared to be in shock. She was frozen in an unnatural position, with her arms over her head and her eyes large and staring.

"What is it, Katie?" Carol repeated anxiously.

"That's just her usual greeting for her father," a clipped voice said from behind her.

Carol spun around on the hardwood floor to

find Simon leaning negligently against the door frame. The lines in his face were harsh, but his eyes were sad as they looked over her head at Katie, who was still standing as though turned to stone. When the child suddenly flinched and crossed her hands protectively in front of her he dropped his eyes to Carol. She sat looking from one to the other in bewilderment. This was the first time she had seen father and daughter together, and she was at a loss to explain the tension between them until Simon's words to her that first night rang in her head:

. . . *you might want to ask Katie about it sometime in the future and watch how she reacts. You see, I think she believes I did.*

It was as though he had read her mind. "I think you see now what I meant," he said softly. His words were quiet and composed, but she heard the pain in his voice. If this was always Katie's reaction to him Carol could understand why he had stayed away from the playroom!

Her attention returned to Katie. She had moved back several steps and was practically cowering in the corner. What fears of her father were going through her troubled mind? Carol wondered. And she knew suddenly, without a doubt, that if she could answer that question she would be well on her way to finding out what kept Katie silent.

"Katie," Simon was saying gently, "why don't you go down to Amy now? I need to speak to Carol for a minute." He moved farther into the room, well away from the door, so that she could skirt around him and edge her way past. Never for a moment did she take her eyes off him.

There was total silence in the room as the two listened to Katie's footsteps retreating down the hall toward the back stairs. She never used the main staircase down to the front hall where her mother had been killed, and Carol didn't press her to do so. Sometime in the future, she hoped, Katie would take her there herself.

For several minutes Carol just sat quietly on the floor and watched Simon as he restlessly prowled about the room, picking up a toy here, a toy there, and setting them down again with military precision.

"Well?" he offered at last. "Why don't you say something?"

"We have to talk soon, Simon." He had stopped in front of her and she rose to her feet. She felt at a decided disadvantage when he towered over her. "What happened just now—"

"I know, I know!" He ran a weary hand over his forehead, as though to smooth out the lines there. "It was stupid of me to hope that a week could make any difference, but I watched for a minute from the doorway before Katie saw me and I thought perhaps. . . ." His words trailed off as he swallowed a lump of emotion. How could she have thought for a moment that he didn't love his daughter?

"These are early days yet, Simon," she said gently.

"I realize that." He forced a smile to his lips. "You've established a very nice rapport with her.

Strictly my layman's opinion, of course. Do all children take to you like that?"

"No, not all," she replied ruefully, thinking of the bruised shin she had received from one particularly difficult five-year-old. "But most of them do. It's simple, really. I like children and they know it."

"Do you like big boys, too?" he asked hopefully. The bleakness had lifted from his expression and his smile was genuine. Her nerves began to quiver. He had a way of making a glance seem as intimate as a touch.

"There's nothing of the child left in you, Simon Forbes!"

"And do you keep your compassion only for children?"

The atmosphere in the room had undergone a decided change. For the moment Katie had been banished from Simon's thoughts. Carol didn't need to look very deeply into his eyes to see what lurked in their shimmering blue depths. The need for compassion was not what she read there.

"I'll give you all the *sympathy* you want," she said dryly.

"It's disconcerting talking to you!" he grumbled. "I always have the feeling that you can see right through me. Do you have any idea how difficult it is to plan a seduction while you're being psychoanalyzed by the object of your desire? It's the very devil!"

"Then give up," she suggested callously.

"You wouldn't consider making your job here a nine-to-five one, would you?"

"I'm afraid that being a psychologist isn't something you can cover up like a typewriter and leave at the office."

"You're telling me!"

She couldn't help but smile at the chagrin in his voice. "Look at it this way," she said brightly. "I could be a karate instructor. Think of the fix you'd be in then."

"Well, let me assure you that you have your own very effective methods of self-defense," he said. "Every time I get ready to make a pass I look at you and you make me feel like a bug under a microscope."

"I'm just returning the favor. As I recall you decided I was a butterfly. Now, let's see. What are you?" She tilted her head to one side, looking him up and down. "Ah, yes. A nice shiny black beetle with a hard outer shell."

"Beetle! I'm a tenderhearted little caterpillar!"

"A beetle," she said firmly, enjoying the nonsense. It seemed much safer than the other topics of conversation she could think of.

His grin broadened. "Okay. The beetle and the butterfly. Quite a combination. Care to walk into my parlor?"

"That was the spider and the fly," she reminded him. "And I was under the impression that I *did* walk in—a week ago."

His expression suddenly sobered. "Speaking of spiders, I almost forgot what brought me up here in the first place. We have company."

"Spiders?"

"Yes! My mother-in-law the black widow and her daughter, to be more exact. They arrived about twenty minutes ago."

Carol didn't need his description of his in-laws to tell her what he thought of them. His tightened jaw and the grim look in his eyes gave her a pretty fair notion of his opinion.

"This is the grandmother Katie lived with last year?"

"Yes."

"The one who tried to gain custody?"

"The very same. Madge."

"I'd like to meet her."

"Short of hiding out in your room, I don't think there's anything you can do to avoid it," he said dryly. "From what I gathered from them just now, they plan on an indefinite stay."

The lines of concern had returned to his face as he shot her a quick glance.

"What is it, Simon?"

"Look, Carol, I know I didn't make things easy for you in the beginning—about coming here, that is—but I would appreciate it if you would . . . well, if you wouldn't mention that to Madge when you meet her."

She stiffened at the implication in his words. His concern touched her professionally as well as personally. She would never have dreamed of betraying what she considered to be a confidential matter between doctor and client.

"I'm not given to blabbing private matters to strangers," she said coldly.

His eyes narrowed at her tone and he examined her face for a moment. "All right," he said at last. "I apologize."

"Apology accepted," she said stiffly.

He waited until the angry color in her cheeks

had faded; then a rueful smile twisted his lips. She found it impossible not to respond.

"Forgiven?" he coaxed.

"Oh, all right. Forgiven."

"Good. Because there's something else I want to ask of you."

"What?" she asked warily, disliking the mischievous expression in his eyes.

"I was just hoping that tonight over dinner you might tell Madge exactly what means you're using to treat Katie, what you consider her progress to be, that sort of thing. Blather on—in strictly professional jargon, of course—about the therapy or anything else that will convince her that any hopes she has of taking Katie back to Philadelphia with her are useless."

"You think that's why she's here?"

The mischievous light faded into grimness. "I know it is," he said curtly. "In her appeal to the judge she made it perfectly clear that she didn't think I was a fit person to raise her granddaughter. She's here to gather evidence to confirm my incompetence. And yours!" he added. "I thought you ought to be forewarned."

"She must love Katie very much," Carol said carefully.

His eyes took on that hooded expression that so effectively hid what he was thinking. "I'll let you judge for yourself," he replied cryptically. "But as for me, I wouldn't willingly put one of my dogs in Madge's clutches, let alone my daughter! Now, make what you like of that, Dr. Durand!"

Carol could make a lot of it. The coldness in his voice was a little frightening and she made a mental note to tread warily where the subject of his mother-in-law was concerned. Still, his obvious antagonism piqued her professional interest. This was something she needed to find out more about and she was actually pleased that the grandmother had arrived. Her relationship with Katie had to be important.

"Gone to sleep on me?" Simon asked, interrupting her thoughts.

"What? Oh, no. I was just thinking."

"I can see that you're simply overwhelmed by my presence. Have I told you lately how hard you are on my ego? I'm just waiting for the moment when you start in on your questions again."

"Is that why you've been avoiding me for the past week?"

"Avoiding you? Nonsense!"

"You have to admit," Carol said, "that since the night of my arrival you've either been preoccupied or absent."

"Do I detect a note of censure in your voice? Don't tell me you've missed me!" he teased, and then added quickly, "Never mind. I don't think I want to know!"

"We have to talk, Simon. Soon."

"Yes," he sighed. "Madge's arrival has rather precipitated the issue."

"Now, then?"

"Not now!" he said firmly. "I've got to spend some time gathering together what's left of my self-confidence so that I can cope with Madge tonight."

He looked self-confident enough to her! Carol thought wryly. He sat poised on the edge of the piano bench like a panther waiting to spring. She couldn't imagine any woman being able to get the better of him.

Suddenly their eyes met and she knew that it wasn't the thought of his mother-in-law that gave his that particular bright gleam. For a moment his guard was down and Carol read there what he would probably have preferred to conceal. There was only one way to interpret the burning glint as his glance raked down over her slim figure. It smoldered with sexual tension.

"You're doing it again," he said softly.

"What?" she asked, suddenly a little breathless.

"Reading my mind. I wish I could read yours."

His eyes searched her face and she quickly lowered her lashes, unsure exactly what it was that she didn't want him to see.

"Want to strike a little bargain?" he asked abruptly.

"A bargain?"

"Yes. I was suddenly wondering why the advantages should all be on your side. How about you answering some of my questions? A little dose of your own medicine, Doctor."

"You mean that you want to do a little poking and prying into my personal life, is that it?"

"With the understanding, of course, that if you answer my questions, I have to answer yours." The smile he gave her was a challenge. "Is it a deal?"

What he was suggesting was certainly unorthodox, but then, Simon was not a conventional man. He made his own rules.

"All right," she agreed before her better judgment could assert itself. "Ask me anything you want—within reason—and I'll do my best to answer."

"I'm going to enjoy this." He grinned.

"Oh, stop gloating and start asking!" she said balefully.

"Right! Age?"

"Twenty-eight."

"Height?"

"Five foot four."

"Weight?"

"One hundred and ten pounds."

"Nude?"

"What?" she asked, startled.

"One hundred ten pounds with or without your clothes on?" he drawled.

"Oh! With."

"See how easy I'm making it for you?"

"Yeah!" she said dryly.

"Birthplace?"

"Boston."

"Are your parents living?"

"No."

"What are your hobbies?"

"Reading, horseback riding, playing the piano."

"Are you sexually active?"

"Wh-what?"

"You heard me."

"Ah, I see," she said. "A little trick question thrown in when my guard was down. You pick up the technique very quickly."

"You haven't answered my question yet!"

"Then the answer is no, not right at the moment," she replied crossly.

"We'll have to see what we can do about that, won't we?" he suggested hopefully.

"Comment unprofessional and out of line, Mr. Forbes!" Carol said firmly. "I think we'd better quit."

"Quit? I'm just getting warmed up, Miss Durand!" He paused for a moment and studied her with narrowed eyes. Then, "Married?"

"No."

"Engaged?"

"No."

"Ever?"

Her hesitation told him more than she would have liked. "Y-yes."

"You broke it off?"

"Yes!" Carol was deeply regretting whatever impulse had put her in this position. Even though she had expected his questions to be direct, she hadn't expected them to be this personal. She should have known better, she thought bitterly. Simon had certainly never given her any reason to suppose he would be reticent about asking her anything he chose!

"You broke off your engagement," he repeated. "Why?"

"It's none of your bus—!"

"Are you going to let me have the same out?" he interrupted. "You ask me a question I don't like and I have the option of refusing to answer?"

"It's not the same thing!" she said through gritted teeth.

"Come on, Carol. Fair is fair."

His mouth had set into a stubborn line and Carol saw that he was in deadly earnest. All traces of humor had left his face as he watched her intently. He wanted her to have a very real sense of just what she intended to put him through. He knew that the questions she would eventually ask him would be every bit as searching and personal, even though her motives would be very different. Well, if this would eventually help save his pride, she would play the game his way.

"All right, Simon," she said quietly, "I'll answer. I was engaged for six months, and then one evening I dropped in on Brian—my fiancé—unexpectedly and found him with another woman. As it turned out, she was just one of many he was lining up to help relieve the boredom of monogamy after we were married. Having a constitutional dislike of running with a herd, I broke our engagement."

She had looked Simon squarely in the eye as she spoke, making no attempt to mask the remembered pain. During the silence that followed she sat stiff and straight on the hard wooden chair, refusing to flinch away from Simon's probing gaze. He would have had to be blind or totally insensitive to miss her pallor or the slight trembling of her lips.

"I'm sorry, Carol," he said quietly. "I've hurt you, and I didn't mean to do that. I was trying to save my own ego at your expense. You didn't deserve that. I know you're only trying to help."

The smile she gave him was genuine, if a trifle wan. "That's all right, Simon. I understood what you were doing. I—I'm just sorry that I'm the one who has to do the asking."

She rose when he did and made no protest when he reached out to smooth a stray lock of hair back over her ear. His fingers trailed along the soft skin of her jaw and rested under her chin.

"That man must have been a fool," he said softly.

Any remnants of pain or chagrin Carol felt faded with those words, and the smile she gave him was warm. He returned that smile with one that parted his lips and filled his eyes with understanding.

"Maybe true confessions isn't going to be so bad after all," he said to lighten the mood. "It seems to have a purging effect. So prepare your ammunition; I'll be ready whenever you are."

The cuckoo clock in the room sounded and Simon checked his watch. "Time to get ready for dinner. By the way, would you dress up tonight, please?"

Carol raised one eyebrow. This was a change. He and she and Ada were usually an odd trio at the dinner table. Carol wore her casual skirts and sweaters because more often than not Simon stayed in his work clothes. Only Ada dressed with any formality.

"Formal?" she asked.

"Formal. Have to convince the in-laws that civilization isn't limited to the big city. Dinner at seven. Cocktails—laced with a little of Madge's vitriol—at six."

"Simon?" She stopped him as he turned to go. "I'll do my best tonight."

"I'm sure you will. You must know that I love Katie more than anyone else in the world and I'll do anything to keep her!"

His eyes had darkened with anger and concern and her hand reached out to him of its own accord.

"You know I'll do anything I can to help."

"I'm counting on it."

The grimness vanished from his face as he took her proffered hand, raised it to his lips and pressed a kiss into the palm. Ten minutes later, when Carol returned to her own room to change, she could still feel the heat of Simon's mouth against her skin.

Just before six Carol took one last look at herself in the ornately carved full-length mirror that stood beside the dresser. On impulse she had included two long dresses in her wardrobe. The one she was wearing now—a soft turquoise crepe —was the simpler of the two, but she wasn't sure she was pleased with the choice. Narrow straps secured a neckline that dipped low in front to reveal a generous amount of cleavage between her high, firm breasts. The gown itself was loosely cut, skimming its way down her slender body to the floor, but somehow it managed to touch in all the right places. She turned to see the back. The crossed straps did little to conceal a large expanse of bare skin and the slit extended well above the bend in her knee.

The memory of the unguarded look she had seen in Simon's eyes that afternoon brought a flush to her cheeks. If he could look at her like that when she was wearing faded jeans and a sweater, what could she expect from him when he saw her in this dress?

Once again she turned to face the mirror. Except for feeling gratitude that she had never needed to diet to maintain her figure, Carol had never given it much consideration. Now she examined it critically, trying to see herself through Simon's eyes.

The blush deepened in her cheeks as she realized that just the thought of his gaze upon her had hardened her breasts, pushing the nipples against the soft fabric. Her body was telling her something that her mind had refused to acknowledge. She was far more attracted to Simon than she had been willing to admit. She wanted to see that special glow come into his eyes when he looked at her. And yes, she wanted a repetition of the kiss he had given her that first day when she had arrived on the island!

A frown marred the smooth line of her brow. Rick's crude comment about her sexuality still had the power to bring her pain. Was she *using* Simon, trying to prove her femininity to herself, or was there something special about his attraction that stirred deeper feelings? She didn't know. Whichever, she was beginning to think that the dress wasn't fair to him. Perhaps she had better change.

Even as she hesitated the choice was taken out of her hands. A knock sounded on the door, followed by Amy's head just poking its way around the edge.

"Simon sent me to fetch you, Carol. It'd be

best if you can come right now. Everybody's down there already but you."

That settled the issue. She took just a moment to change her gold stud earrings for large silver loops and spray a little perfume on her wrists and in the crooks of her elbows; then she grabbed up an embroidered silk shawl that was a deeper turquoise than her dress.

"My, don't you look fine!" Amy cooed, her eyes wide with admiration. The three days they had spent together had cemented their relationship. "You're a whole lot prettier than that Miss Minta." A conspiratorial smile revealed the gap between her front teeth. "She's not going to like it one bit!"

Unconsciously Carol sighed. Minta must be Simon's sister-in-law and Amy's comment didn't sound at all promising for the future.

"Let's go down the back way," Carol suggested as she closed the door of her room behind her. "Then I can just slip in from the breakfast room. I'd rather not make a dramatic entrance if I can help it."

Amy's grin broadened. "They'd notice you no matter where you came from. From what they've been saying, they think you're some old maid with a poker up her back!"

"Oh, dear." Carol sighed again.

"Don't worry, miss. Simon'll look after you. He looks after all of us."

Carol believed her. Simon's household was comprised of a peculiar assortment of servants—from Sam, who did all the odd jobs, to the diligent Ada, who ran the house so efficiently. All of them were absolutely devoted to Simon, and unaccountably it warmed Carol's heart to know that he was able to inspire such love and loyalty in those who served him.

As she went from the servants' entrance to the breakfast room Carol could hear voices raised in the room beyond. Their words were unintelligible, but she couldn't miss the harsh note in Simon's deep drawl or the high, shrill whine of the women's chatter.

They didn't see her slip into the room, so she had a moment to take in the scene unobserved. Her heart leaped as she looked at Simon. He was so handsome! He stood with his back to the fireplace, dressed in a superbly cut white dinner jacket and black pants that emphasized the breadth of his shoulders and the narrow line of his hips. He had shaved since he had left her in the playroom and for once there was no evidence of the familiar clay on his hands.

The two women were seated on the couch in front of him. As yet Carol couldn't see their faces and from the back it was impossible to distinguish which was the mother and which the daughter. Their hair was arranged in elaborate, youthful styles that defied identification.

Beside them in one of the leather armchairs sat Ada, dressed in a gown of emerald green shantung.

"I told you, you can see Katie for yourself tomorrow," Simon was saying. "She wasn't feeling well this afternoon and Amy has put her to bed."

Was that the truth? Carol wondered. Katie had

seemed perfectly all right when she had left her earlier.

"What's wrong with the child?" came the voice on the right.

"Perhaps she heard that you were in the house!" Ada interjected dryly.

"It's about time someone put you in your place!" the woman gasped.

"I've earned my place in this house," Ada retorted pertly. "What have you done?"

"Simon! Can't you shut this woman up?"

"Please, Ada—"

"All right, darling. For *you!*"

"They say that servants learn from their masters," the woman who must have been his mother-in-law continued. "You always were a rude, selfish—"

"You don't have to say it, Madge." Simon smiled coldly. "I know just what you think of me and I assure you that my mother had been married for two years before I was born."

"You have a vulgar, common mind, Simon!"

At that moment he looked up and met Carol's eyes, and she saw the patent relief that shone in his.

"Come in, Carol!" he called, and two heads snapped around to look at her, first with surprise, then chagrin and finally anger. So much for slipping in quietly!

Simon held out his hand to her, indicating that she should join him in front of the fireplace. To present a united front against the two women? His voice as he made the introductions was smooth and urbane, but his hold on her elbow smacked of desperation.

"Madge, Minta, I would like you to meet Dr. Carol Durand, Katie's therapist. Carol, Madge and Araminta Penrod."

"Carol Durand!" Madge said sharply. "Carlton Durand's granddaughter?"

"That's right, Mrs. Penrod. I'm very happy to meet you."

The Penrods' displeasure had not escaped Simon and Carol noted the satisfaction on his face. Had he known what their reaction to her would be? Probably so. Which was why he had asked her to dress up. She had no objection to playing whatever role he had in mind, but the least he could have done was warn her that she would be met with a very feline hostility.

"What can I get you to drink?" Simon said smoothly.

Her glance flickered to the Penrods and back. "Surprise me," she said.

"Haven't I done that already?" He smiled.

"Undoubtedly. Just don't make a practice of it!"

Minta had apparently been ignored longer than she could endure. "What *are* you two talking about?" she asked with a brittle laugh.

The laugh was as artificial as her blond hair, Carol concluded as she watched the girl's eyes rake over her face and down her slim figure with barely controlled rage. Her eyes were a celestial blue, but there was nothing heavenly in their expression. Minta Penrod had definitely taken an instant dislike to Carol, and Carol had to admit that the sentiments were entirely reciprocated.

The girl was probably twenty-three or -four, but she was dressed much more youthfully than her years in a fluffy gown of flowered cambric, overly embellished with ribbons and lace, that did nothing for her mature, well-rounded figure.

"I simply can't believe you're a trained psychologist!" Madge was saying with an edge to her voice that wasn't lost on Carol. "Whatever must your family think?"

"Arthur French thinks very highly of her," Simon said curtly. "We were very fortunate to be able to get her for Katie."

"I have no faith whatsoever in all this therapy and analysis," Madge said blightingly. "There's nothing at all wrong with the child that a little good discipline won't cure! You spoiled her unconscionably, Simon, as I told you over and over again. I raised two daughters of my own, you know, and I know when a child is being deliberately willful."

"And I listened to you, Madge—over and over again! But in a year your methods certainly seemed to have had little effect! Katie is a very unhappy child!"

"And you're saying I made her that way?" Madge's face was threatening to turn an alarming shade of red.

"I'm not saying anything of the kind. I'm just saying that neither of us is expert enough in the field to know what it is that Katie needs. That's why she's here with Carol!"

"So it's *Carol*, is it?" the woman asked archly.

"Are you sure you haven't brought her here for yourself rather than Katie? It certainly didn't take you long to recover from the shock of my poor Angela's death." She made a play of dabbing at her eyes with a lace-edged handkerchief.

Simon was holding on to his temper only with the greatest difficulty. Carol watched his jaw tighten and his eyes narrow in anger.

A defense of Simon came unexpectedly from Minta. "That's enough, Mother!" she said sharply, and then her voice softened with a suspicious sympathy as she turned an artless smile on her brother-in-law. "Of course Simon has to forget that unhappy time. Angie's dead and there's nothing he can do to bring her back."

Carol was startled by the undercurrent of dislike in the girl's voice when she spoke of her sister. Had sibling rivalry survived the grave? Her suspicion hardened into certainty as she watched the expressions come and go on Minta's face. There was a hunger in her eyes when she looked at Simon, a longing that instantly changed a guileless child into a jealous woman. Minta was in love with Simon!

"We were speaking of Katie," Simon interrupted. "She's still my daughter, Madge, and I have the right to determine what's best for her. I had to give you a chance, but I fail to detect any change for the better in her condition. Now I'm going to do it my way!"

"You always were an arrogant, unfeeling creature, Simon! Angie told me often—"

"That will do, Madge!" he snapped. "I'm sure you're not here to rehash my relationship with

Angela and I have no intention of discussing her with you. She was your daughter, but she was my wife! We did not view her in the same way at all!"

"Watch out what you say to me, Simon! I'm not my daughter! I want Katie back and I'm going to get her! You're not fit to have the raising of her!"

"Mother!"

"Be quiet, Araminta! This is none of your concern! You were able to fool the judge, Simon, and you were able to fool Arthur French, but you can't fool me! I'm watching and waiting, and sooner or later you'll make a mistake and I'll have my granddaughter back!"

Chapter Five

*C*arol slipped on the matching peignoir over her beige silk and lace nightgown and shivered. The first chance she had, she would go into Bar Harbor to find a long flannel number that would keep out the cold.

The chime clock on the fireplace struck the hour. Only ten! It seemed two days since she had left her room to meet Simon's in-laws! The evening had been interminable. Shortly after coffee, she had excused herself on the pretext of needing to check on Katie and had simply not returned. At first she had expected a summons from downstairs, but Simon—with a show of fellow feeling—must have recognized that she had endured all she could of his difficult guests.

She shivered again and decided that a fire was

called for. It was much too early to go to bed. She would never sleep, at least not for a while.

Settling down on the braided rug in front of the hearth, she struck a match on the iron grate, held it under the paper on the bottom of Arnold's neatly laid fire and watched it burst into flame. The central heating was inadequate and the fire had been laid for morning, but she would opt for a cold beginning tomorrow and a little cheerful warmth tonight. Goodness knew she needed it after the chilly atmosphere downstairs.

The hostility in the small salon had settled a glaze of ice over the company that had carried over into the dining room. Simon had frozen into a stiff, formal politeness that Minta had been unable to penetrate with all her bright, inane chatter. At last she had fallen into a petulant, wounded silence. Ada, for once in her life, had kept quiet. Madge, too, had seldom spoken, and then only to interject some scathing comment or to direct some pointed question at Carol.

Simon had seen to it that the burden of conversation fell on Carol. He had begun by asking her to explain to Madge the method of treatment she was using with Katie, and by the time they had finished their salads, Carol had felt like a pompous professor, lecturing to a hostile, not overly bright class. Madge's bewilderment at the terms she used—the jargon requested by Simon— rapidly turned into frustrated anger. By the time Amy served dessert Carol was exhausted and visibly wilting.

There were two redeeming factors, she thought

with a chuckle. First, she knew that Simon had been more than pleased with her performance. Once she had caught his eye and seen the wicked gleam of amusement. Second, her monologue had guaranteed that *never* would she be invited to sit down at a meal of Madge's providing. Carol had blown forever her reputation as a desirable, amusing dinner guest. . . .

"I saw light under your door, but you didn't answer when I knocked." Simon's deep voice from the open door made her jump. "May I come in?"

"Yes, of course!" she said breathlessly, her heart still pounding from the sudden intrusion. "I didn't hear you."

"Are you all right?"

Carol had turned on only the bedside lamp, and as Simon closed the door behind him, shutting out the light from the hall, he was suddenly in shadow, making it impossible for her to read his expression, but she heard the note of anxiety in his voice.

"Well?" he prompted when she didn't answer immediately.

"I was trying to come up with the proper reply," she explained dryly. "Do you want a polite answer or the truthful one?"

"Never mind. I think I can guess."

"Let's just say that I'm doing as well as can be expected under the circumstances. It's not too often that I'm invited to a battle and not told to bring my armor!"

"Here I could have sworn that I told you to

dress for dinner," he drawled, strolling into the light of the fire. "And I would say you were as prepared as you could possibly have been. You shot Minta down with her first glimpse of you in that blue thing you were almost wearing."

"That blue thing, I'll have you know," she said, blushing and remembering her own misgivings about the dress, "is an original designer creation of aqua crepe and was very well received at the country club!"

"I just bet it was!"

As he drew nearer she began to rise, but he stopped her. "No, stay just as you are. You're far more approachable when you're all curled up on the rug in that slinky little number. You don't look like a doctor at all!"

In the intimacy of her bedroom, that didn't sound at all safe to Carol! Her pulse rate had increased alarmingly since Simon's arrival.

"Well, then, for heaven's sake sit down yourself," she mumbled. "You—you make me nervous when you—you *loom* over me like that!"

She heard his sigh of relief as he settled down beside her and she realized that if the evening had been hard on her, it had been doubly hard on Simon. His face in the firelight was showing signs of strain and her tender heart was smitten.

"I wish I'd known dress was casual." He smiled. "I would have changed into my velvet smoking jacket. That's some outfit!"

"Sorry you don't approve," she replied breathlessly, stupidly. His eyes were telling her something very different.

His smile deepened, erasing the lines of tension around his mouth. "A man would have to be out of his mind or bound by vows of celibacy to disapprove of that delightful confection of froth and lace!"

"You can take that leer off your face, Simon," she snapped. "I'm more than adequately covered!"

"My dear Carol, hasn't anyone ever told you that sexiness is more often created by how a body is concealed than by what is revealed?"

"And you're the expert."

"Of course!" He grinned. "Suggestion is a far more powerful stimulant than blatant display. If you don't believe me, visit a nude beach."

Carol couldn't help laughing at this rational discussion of such an irrational subject. Gradually she felt herself relaxing. Simon himself seemed much more at ease than she had ever seen him. Apparently their time together earlier had accomplished something after all. He had lost his defensiveness. But then, as a potential nuisance, on a scale of one to ten, she would score pretty low compared with Madge Penrod.

Lazily she stretched, unaware that Simon's eyes were watching the languid movement with both a thoroughly male appraisal and an objective aesthetic appreciation.

"What an unexpectedly nice end to a very unpleasant evening," Carol sighed. The dimness of the room, the flickering light of the fire, the little oasis of warmth there on the rug were creating an aura of well-being and companionship that was very soothing after the tensions and hostilities downstairs. Madge and Minta Penrod were quite a pair! She couldn't help but smile at the memory of Madge's outraged expression when she first caught sight of her.

"Now, what are you thinking to bring that little smile to your face?" Simon asked indolently, and she realized that he had been watching her more closely than she had known.

"About Mrs. Penrod," she answered truthfully.

"And you can smile about her?"

"Oh, I was just thinking that right now I could believe we're the only two nice people in the world."

"I'm honored to be among the chosen," he said. "Honored and more than a little surprised."

"I said right now. Undoubtedly you'll say something to rile me in a few minutes and I'll have to revise my list."

She turned her head and smiled at him—an open, friendly smile of easy rapport.

"You ought to do that more often," he said.

"Do what? Make lists?"

"No. Smile like that."

"Well, you ought to give me more cause!"

"So, it's my fault, is it?"

"Oh, no. I'm not going to quarrel with you and give you an excuse to pick up and leave. We still have to talk. I'm afraid that after meeting your mother-in-law I'm more determined than ever." She hated to introduce an unpleasant topic, but what she told him was the truth. The tensions she had felt in that family circle were not new. She was sure there was a long-standing feud between Simon and Madge Penrod.

"I know," Simon sighed. "I came up here tonight to fulfill my part of the bargain. Then I saw you all soft and sexy and . . . well, I got other ideas."

His eyes strayed to the oversized double bed, already turned down and ready for occupancy. Carol's glance had followed his and she looked quickly away. Relaxation and companionship had suddenly developed into a dangerous intimacy. Time to get back to business.

"Simon," she said quickly, "was Angela like her mother?"

He was silent for so long that she didn't think he intended to answer. When at last he spoke his words were hesitant. "I'm not sure I know how to answer that. I lived with Angela for nearly eight years and I can't really say I ever knew her."

"But you must have loved her once—Angela, that is."

"Did I?"

She glanced quickly at his face and saw that he wasn't being either flip or evasive. He was grim.

"How many men really know the women they marry?" he asked. "Especially in the beginning. Oh, I was infatuated with her. She was eighteen and a very beguiling child. It wasn't until after we were married that I discovered that the woman I thought she was just didn't exist. The girl I thought I knew had been carefully created by her mother."

He fell into a thoughtful silence.

"Simon?" Carol prompted.

"What? Oh, yes. Angela. I thought her name suited her perfectly—an angel! How wrong can one man be?" He smiled wryly, mocking himself. "She was nothing like her mother in appearance. She was dark, petite, blue eyed—just about the loveliest thing I had ever seen. I had just returned from two years studying sculpting in Italy and gone to visit my father in Philadelphia before coming here to live. He had had to move off the island a few years before when his health failed. Anyway, I met Angela at a dance at the country club—I thought by chance."

"It wasn't?"

"No. Madge had set it up with some friends, mutual acquaintances. She had been on the look-out for a rich husband for little Angela since the girl began wearing training bras. And along I came. A good Philadelphia name and a family fortune to back it up." He shot Carol a glance, warm but filled with irony. "Surely you've discovered that inherited money can be a curse as well as a blessing?"

Carol winced. She had discovered that fact all too painfully. And she could well believe what Simon was saying of Madge. The woman had a very predatory air.

"So what happened?"

"What can I say?" He shrugged. "I was ripe for the picking. During my two-year absence my friends had all married and created lives of their own. Marriage looked deceptively appealing. I was easy prey for a scheming mother and a pair of limpid blue eyes. Before the echo of 'I do' had died I found myself tied and bound and supplying Madge with clothes and cars, repaying the mortgage on an expensive house in a select neighborhood, sending Minta to finishing school in Switzerland. . . ."

"Simon, no!" Carol gasped, aghast at Madge Penrod's nerve—or cunning. "Why? Surely—"

"My dear Carol, it's obvious that you've never been harassed by three harping, weeping, plaguing women. In the long run it was far less wearing on my nerves and my pride to give in with as good grace as was possible. Two points, however, I refused to give in on. First, I would not abandon my art for a life of leisure—something that was beyond Angela's pleasure-loving comprehension. And second, I'd be damned if we—Angela and I—would live ten minutes' drive from Madge."

"So you came back here?"

"I gathered what was left of my dignity together, packed up my wife and reopened Porcupine Island."

He spoke so flippantly that she found it impossible to feel sorry for him—which, she shrewdly suspected, was exactly his intention. He wasn't a man to welcome pity.

"Well, is this what you want to hear, Doctor?" he asked dryly.

"Yes, please," she murmured. "Did—did Angela take the move badly?"

"An understatement, my dear girl!" A pained smile curled his lips. "She thought the island was a punishment, that I was reaping some kind of revenge. She didn't love me, you see," he added almost casually, "and she knew that I knew it."

Carol raised an inquiring brow.

"Well, it isn't hard for a man to figure out, Carol," he said, "when his wife suddenly develops severe headaches every night."

"I take it she wasn't ready for . . . er, marriage," Carol said, hoping that she sounded more impersonally professional than she was feeling.

"If by that you mean sex," he growled, "you're right. She never should have left the maternal nest. She viewed the island as her own personal hell. She was lonely, hated the climate, longed for the lights of the city and was terrified of the isolation, the servants, the castle . . . me!"

"You didn't consider moving back to Philadelphia?"

"I'm not pretending I was blameless in the fiasco our marriage became! But within a month I knew I had been made a fool of. Once the first primal urges had been satisfied I found myself saddled with a wife who neither loved nor understood me and whose entire conversation centered around clothes and the fact that I had made it impossible for her to display her vast wardrobe adequately. But, selfishly, I was determined that she would not dictate our life-style or ruin my life!"

"You didn't consider divorce?" she asked hesitantly.

Simon shrugged. "By then she was pregnant with Katie. She must have gotten pregnant on our honeymoon. Some honeymoon! She cringed every time I touched her! But if I got nothing else out of our marriage, I wanted my child. She saw Katie as a financial hold over me, and once the baby was born she informed me that she was taking her back to Philadelphia. I simply told her that she was welcome to try, but I would divorce her on grounds of desertion, fight for custody of Katie and leave her to try to sue me for anything more than child support. I wasn't going to let the Penrods take me for every penny I owned. Oh, no. I had my home and my work and my daughter, and they were enough to give meaning to my life!"

Carol watched the anger and frustration build in him as he talked, and she saw something else in his mobile face, too—pain. Abruptly he stopped.

"Not a very pretty picture, is it? I look back and see myself as a selfish bastard. Do you find it any wonder that these are facts that I would have preferred to keep to myself?"

"Did Arthur know . . . ?" she began hesitantly.

"No! I've never told anyone! And now it has to be *you!*" he added bitterly.

"Simon, I'm not judging you."

"How can you help it, when I'm judging myself?"

"But I'm a doctor, Simon."

"I thought I had demonstrated pretty conclusively that you're a doctor second and a woman first."

"All right, perhaps I am, but I can still see the situation more objectively. You were too emotionally involved to view your home life with any perspective. What I *am* concerned about is what effect your relationship with Angela had on Katie all the time she was growing up. Did your—your wife have any maternal instincts at all?"

At this question Simon frowned and shifted his position on the rug. "Yes," he said slowly. "I think she loved Katie in her own selfish way. She played with her like a child plays with a doll, dressing her up and cuddling her. But she certainly wasn't prepared to make any sacrifices for her."

There was an odd note in his voice that caught Carol's attention. "What do you mean?"

"I mean that there's a real irony in the situation."

"Irony?"

"Yes. On the day Angela was killed, she was going to give me my freedom. She was leaving me for another man."

In spite of all he had been through with his wife, Carol sensed what a blow this had been to Simon's pride. His eyes were a little glazed now as he relived the pain of the past and her heart went out to him. A man, she knew, could often deal with a woman's coldness when he believed it was part of her essential nature, but when he found that another man could give her a pleasure he couldn't, it was humiliating.

"She had met him in Bar Harbor, she told me," he continued. "They had an affair. He was younger than I, equally as wealthy, but far less eccentric, at least according to Angela. At first she threatened to take Katie with her when she left and we had a hell of a row. Ultimately she was far more concerned with her new lover and getting away from me than she was with depriving me of my daughter for the sake of revenge."

Carol remained silent when he paused. He had almost forgotten her presence and she didn't want to break his narrative flow.

"She packed her case and I was to send the rest of her things later," he continued, still seeing the inner vision. "I'd taken the case downstairs and gone to the radio room to call Sam to get the boat ready when I heard the commotion in the hall. By the time Ada and I got there, Angela was dead. She was lying at the bottom of the steps; Katie was with her."

"With her?"

"Yes, kneeling on the floor beside Angela." He paused and swallowed convulsively. "I tried to take her in my arms, but she fought me off and ran to Ada. She's never said a word since."

His eyes returned to Carol, who was sitting now with her arms wrapped around her knees. "Now you know, Carol."

Carol frowned thoughtfully. "And you've never spoken to anyone about Angela's leaving? Not even Madge?"

"No. Angela was dead. Madge had enough pain to endure and I couldn't see adding to it." A rueful smile lightened his expression. "That's not entirely true. Madge would have been furious with Angela for leaving me, and with me for allowing her to go. You see, another marriage was not a part of Angela's plans, and Madge wouldn't have taken kindly to having her meal ticket ditched. Coward that I was, I couldn't face bearing the brunt of my mother-in-law's wrath."

"I don't find that cowardly at all," she said firmly. "If anything, I would say that you used admirable restraint."

For several moments Simon stared into the fire; then he rose to put on another log and watched it as the flames took hold.

"Simon," she asked when the silence lengthened. "Simon, did you mind confiding in me all that much? What you told me tonight is very important if I'm to help Katie."

"And that's all it meant to you?" he said bleakly. "A man bares his soul to you and it's just all in a day's work."

"I didn't say that!"

"Well, you might as well hear the rest of how I feel—so you can write it up for your case records, of course." He ignored her murmur of protest. "Sometimes in my wilder flights of fancy I imagine Angela residing happily in hell laughing at me. She paid me back tenfold for any injury my pride or stubbornness did her. She had her revenge. I don't know how she did it, but when she died she took Katie away from me! In the end, she won!"

Before he turned his head away from the firelight Carol saw a sorrow on his face that nearly devastated her. Here was a man who had lost—psychologically and emotionally, if not in fact—the most important person in the world to him. She had taken Katie's case as she took any case, with a determination that if it was humanly possible she would find a way to cure Katie's illness. But now, more than anything else in the world, she wanted to give Simon back his daughter, happy and emotionally healthy.

If Arthur could have known what she was thinking he would have had a good deal of stern advice about the mistake of becoming personally involved with her clients, but it was too late for that now. She *had* become personally involved—not only with Katie but with her father—and she would be making a bigger mistake not to recognize that fact.

No matter how Simon felt about what he called her poking and prying, his confidences had done him no harm in her eyes. If anything, her admiration for him had grown. She knew the pain and chagrin he had experienced at having his past dredged up. She had felt the same way that afternoon. Wounded pride so often took longer to mend than any physical injury. But Simon had put Katie's welfare first and Carol believed implicitly in his honesty. He had told her the truth—at least, as he perceived it—about his relationship with his wife. Many men, she knew, would have tried to use such a story to their advantage with a woman, making a bid for her sympathy. Simon had used no such ploy.

The intensity of her feelings for him at that moment frightened her a little. There had been none of the usual man-woman easing into a relationship for her and Simon. She knew little about his likes and dislikes, nothing about his tastes in music and books, and he knew nothing about hers. Yet in one day they had come closer, progressed further along the road to discovery, than many couples did in months.

The smile that curved the lovely line of her lips as she looked at Simon was warmer and more intimate than she realized. She heard his sharp intake of breath and saw his hand reach out to her. It was an overture she could not refuse. Her eyes locked with his and her heartbeat began to quicken.

"I've tried to stay out of your way this past week, Carol," he said, his voice husky, "and not just to avoid your questions. I've lived a lonely life here on the island, and I'm no celibate. Do you have any idea what it does to me to see you in my house, at my table, playing with my daughter? Do you have any idea what it did to me tonight seeing you in that dress, looking so indescribably lovely? Do you have any idea what you're doing to me right now?"

How could she answer when his own presence was stirring longings in her that had been dormant for nearly a year? His rugged attractiveness was almost tangible. She wanted to reach out and touch it, savor the feel of desiring and being desired. Oh, this was all happening too fast! The day had been too filled with tension and she didn't trust her own reactions!

Fortunately Simon didn't expect an answer.

"If you knew how much I've been dreading this conversation," he continued. "I knew it had to come, and there were moments this past week when I almost hated you for forcing me to resurrect those bitter memories. And then I told you the whole sordid story and I looked at you, expecting to see contempt or, at best, pity, but instead you *smiled* at me—and such a smile!"

That smile grew shaky as she read the intention in his eyes.

"The truth couldn't harm you with me, Simon," she said breathlessly as he drew nearer and nearer.

"I find that hard to believe," he whispered, his lips a mere inch from hers. "Convince me!"

He waited, and it was she who moved the deciding inch to bring her mouth to his. She could no more have stopped herself than she could have stopped the blood from coursing through her veins. The kiss was long and sweet, with only their mouths touching. Gradually she felt the pressure of his lips increase and her body eased back to lie upon the rug. Still he touched her with nothing but his mouth, his body supported on either side of her by his strong arms. Gently his lips moved to her cheek, to her eyes, to the spot where her pulse throbbed in her temple, then back down to the corner of her soft parted mouth. They stayed there until, in frustration and need, she turned her head to capture his mouth with hers.

Their kiss deepened and he lowered himself against her. She could feel the starched stiffness of his shirt through the thin silk of the negligee that covered her breasts.

"Carol," Simon murmured. "Carol!"

Abruptly he raised his head. "What was that?" he asked sharply.

Suddenly the mood was broken and Carol's first

sharp pang of regret gave way to relief. Her control had nearly snapped and she trembled at the thought of what could so easily have happened there in the intimacy of her bedroom. Would Simon have stopped? She looked at the lines of experience etched in his face. No, he probably wouldn't have. Oh, he wouldn't have forced her, but she certainly hadn't shown herself to be unwilling, she thought with chagrin, and as he had said, he was no celibate! She writhed at the thought of what an easy conquest he had almost made.

"There it is again," he said.

"What?"

"You didn't hear anything? I thought I heard a noise coming from Katie's room."

Carol was happy to use this as an excuse to escape from Simon's disturbing presence and regain her composure. "Let me go and see if she's awake."

She wasn't pleased to find that her legs were still a little shaky as she rose to her feet and quietly entered Katie's room next door. She had checked on the child when she first came upstairs and had left the connecting door open. Earlier Katie had been curled up in the center of her canopied bed, her breathing deep and regular. Now the covers were in a shambles. Her too-thin legs poked out stiffly from her rumpled nightgown. Though she was still asleep she clutched a stuffed animal almost desperately against her chest.

Carefully Carol straightened the covers and drew them back over her. A strangled sound much like a sob came from between the child's clenched teeth.

"Everything's all right, sweetheart," Carol said soothingly, her voice only a whisper. "Sleep, darling."

She had the satisfaction of seeing the little body begin to relax. Poor little mite. If only, Carol thought, she knew what nightmares were haunting Katie's slumber.

The child's breathing was once again slowing to a more restful rhythm, but still Carol waited, more, she admitted to herself, to find a calm she was far from feeling than for Katie's sake. Simon was waiting for her in the next room and she wasn't ready to return—not just yet.

She was greatly troubled by the fact that she was proving so susceptible to Simon's practiced lovemaking. In the two months she had gone out with Rick she had never responded to his kisses as she had to Simon's. She winced at the thought that it had been she who had made that first move when he had invited her kiss. So foolish. Simon wasn't a man to trifle with and he had told her frankly in the beginning what he wanted from her.

Nervously she bit her lip. She knew what he wanted from her, but what did she want from him? It was humiliating to consider that she might be using him either to boost her deflated ego or to satisfy a strictly physical hunger. She had never taken sexual intimacy lightly, the way many of her friends did. . . .

"Carol?"

Simon stood watching her from the shadow of

the doorway. She had no idea how long he had been there, but his eyes were searching as she joined him.

"Is everything all right?" he asked, his glance straying to Katie's quiet form.

"Yes. Katie had a nightmare, I think, but she seems all right now."

She hesitated for a moment as he moved aside for her to precede him back into her room. She didn't want him to think he could pick up where they had left off. Simon, however, seemed to sense her mood, and the look he gave her was impersonal.

"Are you okay?" he asked, his tone reassuring in its calm.

"Of course." She was glad that the room was too dim for him to read the confusion in her eyes. Why did she find it impossible to think clearly when he was near?

"Well, come back to the fire. You're shivering."

In surprise Carol realized that she was, but it wasn't from the cold. Reluctantly she followed him to the warmth of the hearth and sank gracefully onto the rug beside him. For several moments they were silent, pursuing their own thoughts. Idly Carol twisted a stray lock of hair around one finger as she stared into the flames.

What was Simon thinking? she couldn't help wondering. He seemed so relaxed, as though their little interlude had never taken place. The silence between them had lengthened into several minutes, but it was a companionable quiet. Unable to resist the impulse, she looked at him to see if she could tell what thoughts were occupying his mind. She was disconcerted to find that he was openly staring at her with an arrested expression in his eyes. It was very different from any look he had given her before—neither impersonal friendliness nor the half-seductive challenge that she might have expected. His eyes held appraisal intensified by suppressed excitement.

"What's the matter?" she asked shakily. "Have I got a spot on my nose?"

"No." He laughed. "I was just struck by a brilliant idea. Will you model for me?"

"Wh-what?" Surely she hadn't heard him right.

"I want you to pose for a statue for me. I have in mind exactly what I want. I·don't know why I didn't think of it before!"

"Well, I don't want to hear about it!"

"Does that mean the answer is no?"

She stared at him in disbelief. "Simon, I've seen your work! You couldn't possibly expect me to pose—to pose . . . well, for something like that," she finished lamely.

"Now, I wouldn't have thought a psychologist would boggle over a perfectly natural term. You mean you couldn't pose in the nude."

"All right, yes! I can't pose in the nude!"

"Why not?" His voice held nothing but polite interest.

"Because I'm a doctor," she said, driven.

"I've tried to tell you, Carol, that your being a doctor does not preclude your being a very beautiful woman."

"That is not the point!" She rose, but Simon remained on the floor, reclining on one elbow.

"Then why don't you tell me what is?"

"Oh, if you don't understand, I'm not about to try to explain!"

"My, my," he tutted wickedly. "For a psychologist you certainly do seem to have a lot of hang-ups. Do you mean to tell me that no man has ever seen you nude?"

"I don't mean to tell you anything!"

"You have nothing to be ashamed of, you know," he added conversationally. "Your figure is just about perfect. Narrow sloping shoulders, hipbones not too prominent, high, firm breasts—pear shaped and just slightly tilted up—"

"Stop it! You—you can't possibly know that!" His calm, matter-of-fact description was making her tremble with a familiar weakness and she felt the flush of color begin in her neck and spread upward to her cheeks.

The flush deepened as he said gently, "Oh, yes, I can. Your negligee is very sheer and you're standing in front of the fire."

It took her a moment to grasp what he was saying. Then she understood. The firelight from behind made a silhouette of her body through the thin fabric. With a gasp she sank back to her knees. Their relationship had come too far too fast this evening. She had thought she was beginning to understand him pretty well, but this new proposal of his had taken her by surprise. Did he seriously want her to model for him, or was this just a new approach to seduction?

"Do you ever wear your hair down?" he asked.

"Wh-what?"

"I asked if you ever wear your hair down."

"Yes—no!"

"Well, make up your mind."

"Simon, please! I'm not going to model for you!"

"I can't promise you would be as famous as *Venus de Milo*, but I could promise you a good deal of exposure—"

"An unfortunate choice of words, Simon!" she interrupted with asperity.

"You're right!" He laughed, a laugh more carefree than she had ever heard from him. "I must be slipping."

"Well, how about slipping right on out the door?" she suggested hopefully. Time for a strategic retreat. She no longer felt she had control of the situation.

"Well, I can see that you aren't in the mood to talk business tonight. We'll postpone our discussion until another time—"

"We'll put it off permanently!"

"Now, that's asking too much from an artist. But I'm too much in your debt to argue with you."

He had risen to leave and Carol walked with him to the door, careful to keep the shadows at her back. "I hope you don't think you owe me anything, Simon," she said, grateful for a turn in the conversation.

"Well, allow me to thank you anyway. You did very well with Madge tonight. I don't think I've ever seen anyone get the better of her. I'll do my best to see that both you and Katie see as little of her as possible."

"Was Katie really feeling ill?"

"Yes!" he said with a return of his former bitterness. "Oh, she was fine until Ada told her her grandmother had arrived. Keep a close eye on Katie while Madge is here, Carol. I know you only have her for a few hours a day, but I would appreciate it if you would stick close. Don't ever—and I mean *ever*—leave her alone with her grandmother!"

Carol knew an order when she heard one, but she wasn't at all inclined to argue.

"Does the same hold true for Minta?"

He frowned thoughtfully. "Minta? I don't know. She's inclined to be silly and spoiled, but I would think she's harmless enough."

Oh, how furious the girl would be if she could hear that description! Carol thought. Did he know that Minta was in love with him? Listening to him, she didn't think so.

Simon stopped with his hand on the doorknob. "Sure you won't change your mind?"

"About what?" she replied, her thoughts still on Minta.

"About modeling for me. I'm very good at my job. See, no false modesty!" he added meaningfully.

"Much too good!" she retorted blightingly. "I can't imagine that you don't have women fighting for the privilege of modeling for you."

"Ah, but none of them have that certain quality you possess," he said provocatively.

"And just what is that?" she inquired before she could consider the wisdom of such a question. Fortunately—or was it unfortunately?—he chose not to answer.

"That's something I won't tell you until the time comes."

"The time will never come!"

"Ah, but I've piqued your curiosity, and besides, I'm a very determined man, as I once told you."

"Well, you know what they—whoever they are—say about curiosity," she observed tartly.

"Yes, and you know what happened to Pandora. She couldn't resist knowing."

"And thus let loose all the ills of the world on mankind in the process. I hope I wouldn't be so foolish."

"You're a woman, aren't you?"

"Implying what?"

"Oh, no! I'm not going to quarrel with you tonight!"

She glared at him but held her tongue.

"Well?" he asked hopefully after a moment. "Aren't you going to try for the last word?"

"I admit defeat," she said quickly. She was beginning to think she was no match for Simon's quick wit, and the warm smile in his eyes was once again doing very dangerous things to her. Her head told her to get him out of the room—fast! Her body, however, had a will of its own. Unconsciously she swayed toward him and that was all the invitation Simon needed. He reached out and slid his hand beneath her chignon, stroking the nape of her neck.

"You're not defeated yet, Carol Durand," he said softly, pulling her hard against his chest. "When I finally get you to let your hair down for me—willingly—*then* you'll know you're defeated. Go to sleep on that thought!"

Her breasts were almost painfully hard as they pressed against him, and she could feel the quick rise and fall of his chest and the heavy beating of his heart. In her bare feet she felt very small and twice as vulnerable as she had before. Oh, the need, the hunger, were stirring in her again!

Dizzily she looked up into his eyes, and even in the dim light she could see the depth of color there. Was that her own flushed face she saw reflected?

She had no more time to consider as his mouth approached hers, the soft warm flutter of his breath mingling with her own. Slowly her eyes closed and her lips parted. She could taste the sweet, heady elixir of desire on the tongue that probed and teased her own, and she could not restrain herself. Her arms rose to slip up and over his broad shoulders and encircle his neck. Guiltily she savored the pleasure of his nearness as she felt his body slide rhythmically against the slick silk of her robe.

The fires he had lighted in her earlier flared back into life. Her gasp of pleasure was swallowed by those seeking lips as his free hand rode smoothly up the soft robe to explore the lush contours of her breasts. Gently he kneaded and caressed the flesh until the hard nipples were pulsing with desire and her whole body was trembling with aching need.

"Please, Simon! Nooo," she moaned in distress.

"Shhh, it's all right, Carol. It's all right."

For a moment more he simply held her, his nearness now soothing and reassuring her. At last he moved her away, the hands that had minutes before aroused her offering only support.

"You have a beautiful body, Carol," he said softly. "And I'm going to see it all very soon. *I'll* go to sleep on *that* thought!"

Chapter Six

$\mathcal{A}$ clattering of wood awoke Carol the next morning. She yawned and stretched with a sensual abandon. She had been dreaming about Simon. Quickly she retreated under the covers as the shock of the cold air brought her fully awake and drove her dreams back into her subconscious.

"Morning, miss," Amy said brightly from beside the fireplace. "I'll have this fire laid in a jiffy. Coffee's right there on the stand."

"Where's Katie?" Carol asked quickly.

"She woke up a half hour ago and I took her down to eat in the kitchen. Mrs. Penrod left instructions for breakfast in bed at ten."

"And Minta?"

"Well, she wanted to know what time Simon ate his breakfast. I told her sometimes six, sometimes eight, and sometimes he just didn't eat at all." Her voice was bland, but her eyes were knowing as they met Carol's. The girl might be very shy before you got to know her, but there was a lot of street savvy inside that head.

So Minta was going to try to catch Simon at breakfast, was she? One part of Carol—the cowardly part that disliked unpleasantness, especially before breakfast—was ready to forgo the morning meal. But another side of her—the one that viewed the world with an ironic eye—was interested in watching Minta operate. Carol was fairly certain from what she had seen the night before that Mama Penrod was ignorant of Minta's feelings toward her brother-in-law.

Carol quickly drained her cup of tepid coffee, took the time for a quick shower and turned her thoughts to clothes. She dismissed the impulse to put on a dress and instead chose her jeans, a long-sleeved plaid blouse and a suede vest. A pair of stacked-heeled cowhide and lizard-skin boots completed the ensemble. Urban cowboy chic—or "cow hip," as one eastern newspaper had called the trend in western fashions. She wasn't going to try to compete with the soft, fluffy Minta for cutesiness.

As she sat before the mirror and took out the pins that held her now flattened and disordered chignon in place her dream and the memory of Simon's comment about her hair merged. Her hands trembled as the fantasy surfaced from the twilight shadows of her mind. Her hair had been down. . . .

Honestly, she thought crossly, pushing the memory away and shaking her long hair loose.

Sometimes being a psychologist was the very devil! If she had gone into some nice straightforward profession like teaching math she wouldn't have the specter of Freud nipping at the edges of her subconscious!

What made it worse was that she was proud of her hair. She hadn't had it cut since she was thirteen and now it fell wavy and long past her waist. And Sam had been right. The pale ash blond did not owe its color to any bottle.

Brian had liked it down. . . . The thought gave her pause and she tried it again. Brian had liked it down. Brian! For the first time in a year the shooting pain that had invariably accompanied the thought of him was gone! Had Simon been right about the purging effect of their conversation? Was she really free of Brian Castle at last?

Her spirits rose as she rewound her hair and pushed the pins into place. She refused to give herself a final once-over in the mirror. It was her mind that needed to be razor sharp, not her appearance. What she didn't suspect was that the sleek hairdo and casual western clothes did nothing but emphasize the classically regular bone structure of her face and the very feminine, nicely rounded curves of her figure. Unknowingly she wiggled just a little as she walked, setting the designer label on her jeans in provocative motion.

"Good morning," she said cheerfully as she entered the small informal dining room. "How are you, Minta?"

Minta's face had brightened at the sound of her firm footsteps on the slate floor, but it darkened with ludicrous speed when Carol appeared in the doorway. The large shining smile that revealed both rows of teeth froze in place and the eyes that had been peeping through long lashes with a contrived shyness now narrowed ominously.

"Where's Simon?" Minta snapped insolently.

"He was showering when I left him," Carol said sweetly. "He ought to be down in a minute!"

Minta's mouth fell open and then snapped closed into a hard, outraged line. "When you left him—!"

"Oh, for heaven's sake, don't be a sap!" Carol laughed. "I haven't seen him since last night. How should I know where he is?"

The color that had faded from Minta's face now flooded back in anger. "Just who do you think you're speaking to?" she snapped.

"Do you know, I could have sworn that we met last night," Carol said innocently.

"That's not what I meant and you know it! I'll have you know I'm a guest in this house, while you're nothing but . . ."

"Nothing but what?" Carol prompted mildly.

"An employee!" Minta finished. She couldn't have made the epithet sound more insulting if she had said that Carol was a thief.

"But not employed to take rudeness from you, Minta," Carol said dryly, more amused than offended by the airs the girl adopted. This hadn't been a very felicitous beginning to their relationship, she thought.

Fortunately, at that moment Simon put in an appearance, and Minta's whole demeanor underwent a lightning-quick change. The smile was back on her lips, the narrowed eyes now took on a provocative appeal and the high color on her cheeks became a flush of pleasure. But to Minta's chagrin Simon barely gave her a second glance.

"Morning!" he said curtly, and then to Carol, "Have you seen Katie yet this morning? I checked her room and she's already up."

"Arnold has her in the barn with the dogs, and then Amy is going to give her a little exercise." Carol saw him relax. He must have been afraid that the child was with Madge.

"When am I going to be able to see Katie, Simon?" Minta asked, trying valiantly to recapture his attention. "I've missed her so much. We became so close this last year. Why, it was like giving up my own child when she left us."

"She'll be joining us for lunch," Simon said with a casualness that ignored the implication of her words.

"But I thought I could spend some time with her this morning!"

"She works with Carol all morning," he said in a voice that did not invite interference.

"And what are *you* going to do this morning?" she asked hopefully.

"Work."

"Oh, I'd love to watch," she breathed.

"You know I never let anyone watch me while I work," he replied uncompromisingly.

"But surely you could make an exception just this once," Minta pleaded, batting her eyelashes at him in a manner that was meant to be appealing but looked more as though she had something in her eye. "I'd be quiet as a mouse! I'd just sit and not say a word."

He was looking cornered and Carol took pity on him. "If you'd like," she intervened, "you're welcome to join in my session with Katie. You understand that you couldn't just watch—that's inhibiting—but you could play the games with us."

Minta was caught. From the look on her face the last thing in the world she wanted was to spend the morning playing childish games, but on the other hand, to refuse the invitation would tear the devoted-auntie image.

"Now, that's a good idea!" Simon said heartily. "That will give you a chance to see Carol at work. She's very good." Which was the last thing in this world Minta wanted to hear!

An hour later Carol was deeply regretting the offer. Not even the memory of Simon's smile of appreciation was adequate compensation for having to endure Minta's presence in the playroom. The therapy session was not a success. When Amy delivered Katie to Carol's care the child had taken one look at Minta and hidden behind Amy's wide cotton skirt. Minta had spoken to her pleasantly enough, but in a sickly, patronizing voice, as though her niece were not just young but mentally deficient as well.

"Come on, sweetums! Come give your auntie Minta a big bear hug!"

Which was enough to drive the child out of the folds of Amy's skirt and into Carol's arms for protection from her aunt. The look on Minta's face confirmed Carol's every suspicion. The

woman had no more liking for Katie than she had
for children in general. She simply saw her niece
as a means to an end—the end being Simon.

Katie flatly refused to participate in the games
and exercises, but as was Carol's method, she
didn't allow this to prevent her from continuing.
She forced Minta to join her in various activities
until, after a half hour, the woman had had
enough and flounced from the room hot and
flustered. As the door closed behind her Carol
caught a look of satisfaction on Katie's face. Their
gazes met and for the first time she saw a twinkle
of humor in the child's bright blue eyes. A small
conspiratorial smile curved her little bow-shaped
mouth.

"Do you know what I think, Katie?" Carol said
with an answering smile. "I think you're a little
imp!"

An hour later Carol was given the opportunity
of seeing Madge and Katie together for the first
time. Madge arrived under full sail, not bothering
to knock on the door, the fragrance of expensive
perfume trailing after her like an invisible entou-
rage.

"Katie, darling!" Unlike Minta, she did not
invite the girl to hug her but took it as her right.
Carol watched the child's body stiffen as she
turned her face so her grandmother's kiss fell
upon her averted cheek. Madge refused to recognize this sign of rejection and hugged the girl
close before holding her away at arm's length.

"Darling! What have they done to you?"
Madge exclaimed in irritation. "You look like an

absolute urchin!" She turned accusing eyes on Carol.

For *they* substitute: "What have *you* done to her," Carol thought dryly. What she had done to her was get rid of the ridiculous ringlets for everyday wear and pull Katie's hair back in two pigtails tied with blue ribbons to match the casual shirt and jeans she was wearing. Instead of looking like an overdressed doll the child looked like any normal eight-year-old.

"And good morning to you, too, Mrs. Penrod," she said pointedly.

"Uh, yes, of course. Good morning, Carol. You must forgive me. I was just so anxious to see Katie." A pause for effect, then, "Amy!"

The girl had obviously been hovering just outside the door waiting for the summons. In her arms she carried a large box, expensively wrapped with pink metallic paper and a huge bow.

"Katie, darling, I have a present for you."

Katie stood where she was, still watching her grandmother warily.

"Well, don't just stand there, girl. Give Katie the box!"

Amy made no attempt to conceal her dislike of the older woman as she pushed the box into Katie's unwilling arms.

"Open it, darling!" Madge ordered.

Obediently, if reluctantly, Katie sat down on the rug and carefully and methodically unwrapped the package. The printing on the box indicated that it had come from a very chic store and Carol knew that whatever was inside hadn't been purchased cheaply. Madge's irritation grew as Katie put the box aside and slowly began to fold the paper, preserving the bow and winding the ribbon into a neat roll.

"Open it, sweetheart!" The endearment had an edge that made Carol clench her teeth. At last Katie took the lid off.

Inside was an elaborately dressed doll that would have brought delight to any normal child— but Katie was not a normal child. Reluctantly she lifted the doll out under her grandmother's watchful eye.

"There are more clothes underneath," Madge said, pride and satisfaction in her voice at the munificence of her gift.

Either Katie hadn't heard, or she chose to ignore the implied command that she investigate the box further. She simply set the doll aside on the floor and rose to return to the table where she and Carol had been painting with acrylic paints when they had been interrupted.

"Simon told me that she was much improved," Madge said sharply, accusingly, as she turned to Carol. "It seems to me that, if anything, she's much, much worse! Why, not once has she even looked me in the eye, and I've never known her to be rude before!"

"Shall we discuss it later, Mrs. Penrod?" Carol asked with the pleasantness that she adopted with difficult clients. "Katie may not be able to speak right now, but that doesn't mean that she doesn't have a very acute sense of hearing and a superior understanding."

Madge was visibly affronted. "Do you think I

don't know that my own granddaughter is a very intelligent person? That doesn't mean, however, that I am willing to condone such behavior to her elders! The child is perfectly capable of learning good manners. I would never have tolerated such rudeness while she was in my home."

I just bet you wouldn't, Carol thought. Which, of course, was why Katie was cowering over her painting as though her life depended on it!

"It was very nice of you to come to see Katie," Carol said pointedly. "We have another half hour of work to do here and then I'll bring her down to the small salon. She'll be eating lunch with us and that will give you a chance to talk with her."

A dismissal—as nicely phrased as Carol could make it, but a dismissal nonetheless. For a moment she thought Madge was going to give her an argument. The woman's red lips thinned in anger to the point that they nearly disappeared into her face and her cheeks turned an alarming puce.

"I am beginning to see where Katie is learning her manners!" she bit out cuttingly. "I'll have more to say to you later!"

Tension hung over the room for a full two minutes after the door closed behind her. Katie's back was ramrod straight as she slapped paint on her paper with a fevered zeal. The drawing was a figure outlined in black with a pointed hat and a red slash of a mouth across the face, the corners turned down to form a frown: unmistakably the picture of a witch. Carol was left in no doubt as to the way Katie perceived her grandmother.

* * *

In the week that followed, the climate of hostility created by the Penrods intensified and a general air of gloom hung over the household.

Minta's dislike of Carol grew to the proportion of an obsession. She blamed Carol for the fact that Simon ignored her and never lost an opportunity to direct a pointed barb at her. Madge's temper had become shorter and shorter as her frustration increased. She poked and pried into every corner of the house, questioning the servants, snooping in Simon's study and eavesdropping on Carol's sessions with Katie. Simon himself was forced to withstand the worst of her abuse.

Only Katie had escaped her grandmother's acid tongue. After that first encounter in the playroom Katie had been a model of deportment. In her grandmother's company she wore the dresses Madge had provided for her in Philadelphia, and under her arm she carried the detested doll—constantly. Carol had no difficulty recognizing this as a badge of defiance. Madge was not as perceptive, though Carol knew that the woman was far from pleased with Katie's docility. It didn't take her many days to figure out that Madge didn't want the therapy to succeed.

The most positive result of Madge Penrod's presence was Katie's new relationship with her father. The child's instincts for survival were acute, Carol concluded. If Katie didn't show Simon any affection, at least she didn't cringe in a corner every time he entered the room. In her

own silent way Katie had joined forces with Carol
and her father against Madge.

Eight days after the Penrods' arrival Carol
restlessly paced her room, her black taffeta dress
rustling in accompaniment to each step. A lock of
hair from her bun came loose and fell across her
cheek. Impatiently she stopped before the mirror
to push it back into place, but her hand paused,
then trembled and finally lay fluttering against her
cheek. She looked like a hag! Her face was pale,
her eyes overly bright, and dark circles like
bruises stood out above her cheekbones.

She hadn't thought the situation could get any
worse, but this evening had proved her wrong. At
dinner Madge's patience had snapped. Katie had
upset her glass of milk, spilling it all over her
grandmother's designer dress. All hell had broken
loose. Madge had slapped her; Simon had roared
with anger; Minta had burst into tears. And
through it all Katie stood stoic and silent, with-
drawing into herself. By the time Carol led her
away Simon had stomped from the room, leaving
Madge to hurl abuses after him.

Oh, Lord! Carol whispered—and it was a
prayer. How much longer could this go on?

The hall clock struck the hour and Carol's body
sagged. Only nine! Much too early to go to bed.
Nervously she bit her lip. What she really needed
was to talk to Simon. They hadn't been allowed
two minutes alone together. Minta constantly
kept her eye on them with paranoid fervor. If
Carol had hoped for a repetition of Simon's visit
to her room her good sense told her that with

Minta right across the hall it was far better that he hadn't come.

Short of a talk with Simon, she concluded, the next best thing for her would be to get out of the house for a while.

The decision made, she quickly changed from her evening dress to jeans and a sweater, pulled on her boots and slipped into her leather coat. At the door to her room she hesitated. She didn't want to chance Minta catching her sneaking out of her bedroom. The girl was likely to put her own construction on where Carol was going, she thought bitterly.

Katie was sleeping deeply when Carol crossed through her room to the playroom beyond. From there she could go out the side door to the service stairs at the back of the house. Carol giggled a little hysterically when she finally reached the deserted kitchen below. She felt like a prowler.

Once she was out the back door and on the wide veranda she felt an immediate sense of release. She hadn't realized how stifling the atmosphere in the house had been during the past week. The night was cold but clear. Just the sliver of a moon lighted the November sky. For a long moment Carol simply stood and breathed the sweet fragrance of pine that permeated the crisp air.

What a beautiful place this was! Except for a small area that had been cleared for a garden the terrain had been left in its natural state. Through the leafless maple, birch and sumac trees Carol could just make out the barn and hen house. Perhaps she would walk over there and visit

Katie's dog Fu and her family. She was fascinated by the big furry snub-nosed chows.

Long slender pinecones crunched underfoot as she made her way along the path. It wasn't until she had rounded the side of the barn that she saw a light burning through the slits in the wood. As she opened the door she felt the warmth of the kerosene space heater and she frowned.

"Sam?" she called. Fu put her nose up over the edge of her wooden box and barked once in greeting while the cow stood eyeing her with calm detachment. "Arnold?"

"Will I do?" asked a deep voice from behind her, and she jumped.

"Simon!"

The hay on the floor had muffled his footsteps and she turned to find him only two feet away. "Honestly, you scared me to death! Why didn't you say something?"

"I wanted to make sure you were alone."

"You thought maybe I had brought Minta with me?" she asked dryly. He grinned in response and she looked around curiously. "What are you doing here?"

"I would guess the same thing as you—escaping! I figured that this was one place where Madge wouldn't be likely to track me down. Come join me," he invited, leading her to an empty stall half-filled with hay.

"I—I don't want to intrude if you would rather be alone."

The tightening of his hand on her arm and the warmth of his smile dispelled any doubts she might have had of her welcome.

"What a week!" Simon exclaimed, pushing her gently down into the hay. "Do you realize that I haven't had two minutes alone with you?"

"But it's been a good week in some ways," she said quickly, knowing exactly what was on Simon's mind. "I've made a lot of progress with Katie."

"There speaks the good doctor," Simon said. "I wonder if you have any idea how chilling it is when you don your white coat—metaphorically speaking, that is. That professional aura is far more effective than a cold shower."

"Simon, I don't—"

"Of course you do! You always feel safer bringing our conversations back to Katie. Who is it you don't trust, Carol? Me, or yourself?"

Much too astute an observation, she thought wryly. She *didn't* trust herself around him, as he suspected.

Nervously she plucked at the hay, her eyes averted from his face until, in frustration, he covered her restless fingers.

"Okay, okay! We'll play it your way for a while. There are just times when I believe I'm almost jealous of the attention and affection you lavish on my own daughter."

"She needs me, Simon!"

"And you think I don't?" he asked whimsically.

"A lot of the barriers she's built up over the year are beginning to come down," she continued doggedly, unwilling to answer his question. "Tonight, when I took her to bed, for the first time she broke down and cried in my arms."

"And we have Madge to thank," he said bitterly. "When she slapped Katie tonight . . . well, we won't go into that. At least I have to give Madge credit for the fact that Katie doesn't run from me now. She looks at me, then looks at her grandmother, and I'm the lesser of the two evils."

"Why on earth do you let them stay on?" Carol asked in genuine puzzlement. "Why do you put up with them?"

"If I had my say I'd kick them out of the house and never set eyes on them again!"

"You don't have the say?"

"That was one of the concessions the judge made. Madge has the right to visit Katie at any time to reassure herself that she is being cared for properly."

"How on earth she was able to get such a hold on you in the first place is what I don't understand. Doesn't a father have all rights over his child?"

"You might call it the work of a very good lawyer and a very thorough job of character assassination," he said dryly. "My reputation as an artist—the kind of work I specialize in—immediately made me subject to suspicion. Couple that with the possibility that removing Katie from the scene of the accident might help and Madge got her own way."

"Oh, I do wish they would leave," Carol sighed.

"Well, I've given you a way to escape them for several hours a day."

"You have?"

"Yes. Model for me. No one invades my studio."

"Simon! I can't!"

"Now you're just being stubborn. I assure you, you would be perfectly safe." He grinned. "I make it a point never to seduce my models. I guarantee that I would see you as nothing but a work of art."

For some reason that thought troubled her even more.

"Do you mean to tell me you aren't physically attracted to your models?" she couldn't help asking.

"Of course I am! I choose my models for their physical beauty."

"But not sexually attracted, then?"

"Come on, Carol. What is sexual attraction if it isn't physical attraction?"

"But physical attraction doesn't necessarily mean physical beauty!" she protested.

"No?" he asked lazily. "Then just what does it mean?"

"Well, it can mean . . ." She shrugged. "Well . . . love."

He took her hand and began playing idly with her fingers. "You use the term too generally," he chided. "I prefer to use it specifically. I *love* your long, slender fingers. I *love* your small soft earlobes, the shape of your mouth, your larger lower lip, your firm breasts—"

"Simon!" she gasped. "Stop it!"

"In fact, I *love* the way each of those parts form the whole, and I would *love* to immortalize that beauty in art."

"Please, Simon! Stop!"

"Why? Why does it trouble you?"

"You wouldn't understand," she answered lamely. She hardly understood herself. All she knew was that she was troubled by something more fundamental than his enumeration of her physical attributes. What troubled her was the look that came into Simon's eyes when he examined her feature by feature, limb by limb, with visions of bronze in his head. In some way it dehumanized her, made her an inanimate object rather than a person.

"You've gone away from me again," Simon said softly and she knew he had sensed her withdrawal.

"I'm sorry."

"No, *I'm* sorry. We won't mention your modeling again. And I have to admit that I have something else on my mind right now."

His voice had turned soft and persuasive and she felt her pulse begin to quicken.

"You—you do?" she breathed.

"Uh-huh."

The coldness that had chilled her when he spoke of modeling melted in the warmth of his smile and the desire she read in his eyes. At that moment both she and Simon knew just how human she was, and she didn't try to stop him when he pushed her gently onto her back in the hay. It was almost a relief to have him his usual seductive self.

"I've waited a week for this," he said softly.

He was doing it to her again, mesmerizing her with a charisma that was his alone. He didn't even have to touch her to send her senses rioting. His glance was an electric spark, his smile a caress, his whole aura of masculine virility and leashed power an aphrodisiac.

"Kiss me, Carol," he whispered.

Carol found herself unable to withstand the appeal in his voice. Truth be told, at that moment she needed his warmth as much as he wanted hers. Her lips found his unerringly and they fused in instant response. She and Simon might have been lovers for weeks, so quickly did they adapt to each other's needs. Her mouth was parted and ready for his exploration. Her body was soft and pliant as he shaped it to fit his own. By degrees the embrace deepened, their kisses lengthening and hardening. His lips on hers became more and more demanding and his arms tightened to hold her against him in a convulsive grip. Carol returned kiss for kiss with her own fierce energy. Her hands tangled in his hair and her body strained to feel his through the thickness of their coats.

Slowly he turned her until he could reach her belt and in a moment her coat was open. Her sweater was no barrier. Easily his hand slipped beneath it to seek out the hot firmness of her breast.

"You're not wearing a bra," he breathed into her open mouth as he teased her lips with his tongue.

"No," she whispered, her back arched as she sought to press her breast more firmly against his palm.

Oh, he was arousing such emotions in her! She knew it was dangerous, but surely a little lovemaking wouldn't do any harm. As he had said, it had been a difficult week, and there was such pleasure in his arms, such comfort.

She buried her face in his neck as he sought the softness of her skin just below her ear. Deeply she inhaled his own personal aroma mingled with the pungent smell of the hay. Gently he nibbled the earlobe he had aptly described just a few moments before and she felt a shiver tremble through her. How strange, she thought dizzily, to be so cold and so hot at the same time.

His chest expanded and then contracted as he expelled a sigh. With one last caress of her breast he smoothed her sweater back in place.

"This is ridiculous, Carol," he muttered. "A thirty-room house and we have to sneak out to the barn like a couple of teenagers!"

Carol couldn't suppress a slightly hysterical giggle. "Don't tell me you used to pick barns for your youthful trysts! I would have pegged you as more the backseat-of-the-car type."

"They both have their drawbacks." He grinned wickedly. "By the time I was old enough to drive I was over six feet tall and backseats were too small and cramped. Barns have the space, but they can be very smelly and cold—especially in November!" He ran a teasing finger down her cheek. "And contrary to popular belief, hay isn't all that comfortable. It can be very irritating to the nude body. The first time we make love I don't want you distracted by a piece of hay poking you in the ear. I'll want your complete and undivided attention!"

Carol was sobering quickly. He spoke of her future surrender with such assurance! She admitted frankly to herself that she had wanted and enjoyed Simon's light lovemaking tonight, had virtually asked for it, even. Subconsciously, did she want their relationship to develop into a full-scale affair?

No! She couldn't be so foolish. She still had far too many doubts about herself and about Simon.

Abruptly she stood up. Her hands were shaking as she retied her coat and smoothed her hair. In irritation she pulled a truant piece of hay from her chignon and threw it on the floor. Simon remained where she had left him, reclining on one elbow in the hay.

"You're shaking," he said gently.

"I—I'm cold!"

"Far from it," he murmured lazily. "Give me the chance and I'll prove it to you."

Their eyes met and she saw that the casualness of his tone didn't match the intense purpose she read there.

"Meet me tomorrow night," he continued softly, "in my studio. All the creature comforts and guaranteed privacy."

"I can't, Simon!" she said a little desperately.

"Can't or won't?"

"Whichever, it amounts to the same thing. I don't want an affair with you!"

"Liar!" he chided.

"I'm going back to the house!" She had to escape from him before he broke her defenses down completely and she agreed to anything. Her desire for him was becoming a torment. "Good night!"

"Good night, Carol. Sleep well."

Small chance of that, she thought as she fled from the barn. She had enough to think about to keep her awake for a week!

Chapter Seven

$\mathcal{I}$ need to go into Bar Harbor, Simon!"

Madge Penrod's strident voice cut through the silence in the sitting room. Carol looked up from the letter she had been reading, the first one from her aunt in the nearly three weeks she had been in Maine. It had been mailed nearly ten days before, but mail delivery depended on Sam's infrequent trips to the mainland. Her aunt, it seemed, was willing to forgive and forget and never mention Rick again if Carol would return to her senses and come home immediately.

"Simon! I need to go into Bar Harbor!"

Simon looked up from the book he was reading and across to where Madge was restlessly pacing the room. It had been a grim morning, the atmosphere decidedly arctic. Since Madge had slapped Katie the night before Simon had given up even the pretense of politeness.

"Did you hear me, Simon?"

"You're a difficult woman to ignore, Madge," he said coldly, bringing angry color to her face. "It's a shame you didn't mention it earlier. Sam just got back an hour ago."

"I was not prepared to leave at dawn! The least you could do is take me over yourself."

Simon turned and met Carol's eyes, his brows raised in inquiry. "Well, how about it, Carol? Do *you* want to go?"

Carol had the horrid suspicion that if she said no, he would refuse Madge's request and bring the woman's wrath down on both their heads.

"Yes," she said quickly. "It's a beautiful day."

"That settles it, then." And he added provocatively, "You're in luck, Madge. We'll go."

"I'm coming too!" Minta piped up from across the room.

"Which delights us all," Simon drawled. "We'll leave in half an hour."

Carol was really very excited about the prospect of the trip. The day was cold, but clear. So far the good weather had held and the November sun, while not really warming, was cheerful. The trek through the woods to the boat harbor was a bit of a trial, however. Neither Madge nor Minta had worn suitable shoes and Minta clung to Simon's arm with a determination that made her wonder if the woman had deliberately chosen the highest heels she owned.

Once Minta was on board she hurried quickly

to the cabin, practically shoving Carol out of the way to secure the place beside Simon for herself.

Well, let Minta have the honors, Carol thought dryly. She herself preferred to sit outside and enjoy the stinging spray from the sea. Unlike Minta and Madge, she had dressed properly for the occasion.

The trip across to Bar Harbor was shorter than Carol would have liked, and once on shore she quickly detached herself from the group. "I know you'll forgive me if I leave you. I want to check on my car and then I have some shopping to do."

She chose to ignore the reproach in Simon's eyes. He was a big boy. If he wanted to get away from the women he was perfectly capable of speaking up for himself.

"You'll meet us for lunch." Not a question—an order.

"Of course. When and where?"

He checked his watch. "Shall we say the Pequod at one-thirty?"

"Right!"

Simon caught her arm as she would have moved past him. "Don't let me down," he said for her ears alone. "I won't be responsible for my actions if I have to eat alone with those two!"

Her lips twitched at the vehemence in his tone. "Don't worry," she said softly. "I'll be there to support you through the ordeal."

He squeezed her hand and stared down into her face. The pleasure of the trip had brought a particularly bright gleam to her eyes. Her hair was all untidy from the wind and color flamed in her cheeks from the cold spray, but the disorder became her.

"Have I told you that you're a gorgeous creature, Carol Durand?"

"Often!" she retorted pertly.

"Well, don't forget it!" He grinned.

"What are you two talking about?" Minta interrupted jealously.

"One-thirty, then," he repeated, ignoring the question.

That gave Carol nearly two hours and she intended to make the most of them. A block down the street she found a clothing store. It catered mostly to the tourist trade, but also carried a small supply of less frivolous items.

Over an hour later she emerged from her fifth store and ruefully readjusted the packages in her arms. She had purchased far more than she had intended. Besides the long flannel nightgown, velour robe and fuzzy slippers, she was now the proud owner of a lovely hand-knit sweater, a sweat shirt with Acadia National Park imprinted on the front and a ski jacket in lemon jellow that she hadn't been able to resist. She would be warm enough anyway, she concluded wryly.

The Pequod, a small rustic restaurant decorated with a whaling motif, was just across the street. She looked up and down the sidewalk for a moment, but saw no sign of Simon or the Penrods. Well, she was fifteen minutes early. Her newly acquired burdens would make any more shopping difficult, so she decided to wait for them in the restaurant.

The deserted foyer was lined with benches. She guessed that in the summer this would be a very popular place, with tables at a premium. The host greeted her cheerily. He was an older man with a shock of gray hair and an equally gray beard. He might well have been a whaler himself at one time, she suspected.

"I'm waiting for my friends," she explained when he approached her.

"Do you want to sit at a table? Or you can just make yourself comfortable here."

"I'll wait here, thank you." She smiled and gratefully surrendered her packages to the man.

"They'll be here behind the counter," he told her helpfully.

Her back was to him as she untied the belt of her coat. She felt hands on her shoulders, but instead of removing the coat they tightened and a voice said softly in her ear, "I didn't think finding you was going to be this easy! A post office box isn't much help!"

She froze, her hands suspended at her waist. "Rick!" she exclaimed without turning.

"The very same! You didn't really think I was going to let you go, did you?"

"How did you find me?" she asked bitterly. There was only one way he *could* have found her. Her aunt!

Slowly she turned to confront him. The host had taken in the situation at a glance and tactfully left them alone.

"Oh, I have my ways," Rick said evasively, and that was all the confirmation Carol needed. Before leaving Boston she had sworn her aunt to secrecy as to her whereabouts, but she should not have underestimated Rick's persuasive powers.

"It doesn't seem to me that I inspire much loyalty in my relatives," she said dryly.

"Now, don't blame your aunt too much." He grinned—the engaging grin that Carol no longer found at all engaging. "She just has a soft spot in her heart for young lovers."

"We're not lovers and we will never be lovers!"

"Ah, but I'm modern enough to believe that if you scratch a good marriage, you'll find lovers underneath."

"I am *not* going to marry you, Rick!"

"Sure you are, baby! I've given you nearly a month to get over your little temper tantrum, but now it's time to come home. That's why I'm here, to take you back with me. When you pick a place to get lost, you don't mess around, do you? What the hell are you doing here, anyway?"

"I'm not going back with you, Rick!" she snapped, refusing to discuss the matter with him. "You might as well leave now so you can get back to Boston before dark—unless you plan on staying and playing the tourist for a while."

"I'm not leaving without you, sweetheart." She knew he was trying very hard to keep his temper, but she saw the telltale signs of anger in his narrowed eyes and forced smile.

"Rick, let's talk about this reasonably and calmly."

"Just what's reasonable about you running away because of a silly little quarrel?"

"It—it wasn't just the quarrel! I had had a lot of doubts that we were right for each other right from the start!"

"Well, you sure didn't act like it, baby!" His anger was growing. "Did you get a kick out of leading me on?"

"I didn't lead you on!"

"No?" he said nastily. "Do I need to remind you of several cozy little evenings we spent together? And what do you call it when all our friends expect us to get married? No one—and I mean no one—has ever dumped me, sweetheart! You aren't going to make a fool out of me!"

Carol's own temper was slowly getting the better of her. Rick didn't give a damn about her; all he cared about was his stupid pride!

As though he read her thoughts, he added quickly, "You know I love you, Carol. You know I'm only thinking of what's best for us."

"Which is why you took me up to your apartment that night, of course," she snapped.

"Yes! I know what you need, even if you don't."

"You made that very plain. I don't know how much you remember," she said icily, "but I remember every word. You had a great deal to say about what my needs are, at least as you see them. What did you call me, frigid?"

"So what of it?" he growled belligerently. "You have to admit that you'd been cold and—"

"I'm not willing to discuss it with you anymore, Rick."

"And I don't want to discuss it either! Talking doesn't prove anything. You're coming back with me!" His anger was dying, replaced by something else. The lust was back in his eyes as he looked at her. She had wounded his pride, but in spite of that he still wanted her.

"Carol, sweetheart," he said, his voice low and husky, "come back with me. Let me love you. Let me make a real woman of you."

"And just what makes you think I'm not a real woman?" She found herself growing angrier and angrier. Why wouldn't he leave her alone?

"You've got a body that's enough to drive a man wild," he continued, ignoring her question. "That touch-me-not air of yours makes me crazy. I've got to have you!"

She could tell that he meant it! Suddenly she had had all of him that she could take. He had hurt her, insulted her, and she wanted him out of her life once and for all! She forced a slow—and, she hoped, knowing—smile to her lips.

"Rick?" she said softly. "Do you think you're the *only* man who's said the same thing?"

"What do you mean?" The arrested look in his eyes told her that her tone had been just right.

"I mean, do you really think that you're the only man who's ever wanted me?"

"Brian . . ." he began, frowning.

"I'm not talking about Brian," she scoffed. "Brian is past history. I'm talking about now."

"I—I don't know what you mean!" He was genuinely startled.

"I mean that you certainly don't believe that you were the only man in my life," she taunted.

"You weren't seeing anyone else!"

"No? Just how do you know that?"

"I—I would have known!"

"I've never been a woman to talk about my lovers with other men," she chided.

"Lovers!"

"Well, lover—singular."

"Who?" he demanded angrily.

"Just what do you think I'm doing up here in Maine?"

"You told your aunt you were working on a case!"

"Well, Cora has a very old-fashioned outlook on life, you know. I could hardly tell her that I had gone away on vacation with a *man*, now, could I?"

"A man! Who?"

"Oh, Rick!" she sighed plaintively. "I've told you before that you're such a bore when you repeat yourself!"

"Who?" he demanded harshly, his fingers biting into her arm.

"You see," she said, shrugging, "I'm not frigid with every man—only you. You just don't turn me on." He would *never* forgive her for that one!

"I said, who?" he snarled.

"You don't have the right to ask that! Now, let go of me!"

Instead he shook her until her head snapped back on her slender neck.

"Tell me who! Who is this lover of yours?"

"All right!" She winced in pain. "I'll tell you, but let me go!"

His hold slackened slightly. "Well?" he demanded harshly.

"Simon Forbes! I'm living on an island with Simon Forbes!"

She heard his quick-drawn breath, and it took her several seconds to realize that the sound had an echo behind her. Rick, too, had heard the gasp followed by a low muttered oath, and his eyes moved from her face to a place just beyond her shoulder.

"Carol!"

Oh, no! she thought, closing her eyes in despair.

"Carol!" Simon repeated from behind her.

Slowly she turned to face him. His eyes were puzzled, his mouth grim, his jaw set. How long had he been standing there? How much had he heard? More than enough, she concluded with a sinking sensation in the pit of her stomach. His presence was bad enough, but a moment later her vision widened to take in the figures of the two women standing on either side of him. Minta stood white and trembling in outraged anger. Madge's expression was much harder to interpret. For the space of several seconds no one said a word and Carol was struck by a hysterical impulse to burst into laughter. They all looked like wax dummies!

Simon's expression, however, sobered her quickly. He was smiling, but his eyes were glittering dangerously. "Carol," he repeated for the third time. "Aren't you going to introduce us?"

"Simon," she said weakly, "Rick Sanders."

"This is Forbes—?" Rick began, but Simon interrupted him ruthlessly.

"Sanders, I'll give you just one minute to get your hands off her!"

"What right have you got to order me around, Forbes?" Rick said belligerently, tightening his hold on Carol's arm.

Simon hesitated only a moment as he met the unconscious pleading in Carol's eyes. "I believe Carol told you what right I have," he said slowly.

"Then you admit that you and she are—are . . ." His voice trailed off in shock.

"I can't see that we owe you any explanation whatsoever," Simon replied curtly. "Now, take your hands off her!"

Carol breathed a sigh of relief as Rick's hands dropped and he took an involuntary step backward. Simon had backed up her outrageous announcement and saved her pride! She shuddered at the thought of Rick's mocking derision if he had discovered her lie. As it was, he looked stricken. Between them, she and Simon had delivered his inflated ego a terrific blow. Not his heart, she consoled her conscience, his ego. But, still, she could almost find it in herself to feel sorry for him for his public humiliation. She hadn't meant for this to happen.

Her sympathy quickly died, however, as she saw the anger begin to gather in his eyes. He had survived the first shock and was starting to recover.

"I don't believe it," he said truculently. "You belong to me, Carol."

"I don't belong to anyone but myself, Rick," she said coldly.

"Not even Forbes here?" he returned nastily.

"I don't look upon a woman as a possession, Sanders," Simon interjected, "but I do know how to take care of a lady. And if you ever—ever—lay a hand on her again, you'll answer to me! Come here, Carol!" She took the hand he held out to her and he pulled her close against his side, his arm around her waist. "Now, get out, Sanders, before I forget that there are women present."

"You haven't heard the last of this, Carol!" Rick blustered. "I don't believe—"

"Out!" Simon roared.

Carol had never seen Rick move so fast. Gone was his fashionable languor. His face turned a mottled red and he kept his eyes averted as he grabbed his coat from the rack in the corner and made for the door.

An ominous silence followed his departure and Madge was the first to break it. "Would you care to explain yourself, Simon?" she said coldly.

"I don't see that I owe you any explanation either, Madge!" His tone matched hers for iciness.

"It isn't really true, is it, Simon?" Minta whined. "That you and she—?"

"Oh, shut up, Minta!" her mother interrupted impatiently. "Of course it's true. You heard her admit it! The little tramp—"

"Madge!" Simon bit out furiously.

"I don't believe it!" Minta wailed.

"Oh, don't be any more of a fool than you can help!" Madge snapped.

"Now, Madge," Simon said coldly, "would you care to take back that statement about Carol?"

"I have no intention of taking it back!" she said

triumphantly. "I knew, of course, that something was going on between the two of you the minute I arrived. *Dr. Durand,* indeed! And that little show you put on of working with Katie! You didn't fool me for a minute! You're just using the child as a blind to hide your own sordid little affair—"

"That's enough, Madge," Simon bit out. "I've taken all I'm going to take from you!"

"You don't have to take anything more from me, Simon. You'll hear from my lawyer."

"Then I suggest that you make plans to return to Philadelphia with all possible speed. I'll have Ada pack your bags and Sam will have them here by morning."

Madge drew in an outraged gasp. "You're turning us out?"

"Did you really think I'd let you set foot in my house again after your malicious accusations? And if you don't like it, take me to court!"

"That's just what I intend to do!"

"Good-bye, Madge! Come on, Carol."

He unconsciously bruised her arm as he practically dragged her toward the door, but Carol made no protest. She knew he was furious and she was stricken with remorse. That whole ugly scene had been all her doing. If only she hadn't allowed Rick to make her lose whatever good sense she had. If only she hadn't been trying to strike back at him for her own wounded pride. If only Simon and Madge hadn't overheard. If, if, if! Too late now for ifs.

"Simon, please!" she panted when he had dragged her nearly a block. "People are staring."

"Let them stare!" he said furiously, but he

slowed his steps to match hers. "Boy, lady, did you let the cat among the pigeons—or should I say peacocks?"

"Oh, Simon, I'm so sorry! We—we can't just leave it like this. Let me go back and explain that I made the whole thing up."

"And do you think for a minute that they would believe you?"

"I'd make them!"

"Not if you swore on a stack of Bibles. Why should Madge believe the truth when you said just what she wanted to hear—and in front of witnesses? Her accusations would hold up in any court in the country."

"I'm—I'm so *sorry*, Simon, if I've made trouble for you! I wish I had had my tongue cut out before I told Rick anything so stupid!"

"You may well wish it before this little episode is finished. It's your reputation, too, you know."

"You don't think it's finished?"

Wishful thinking, she realized with a sinking heart. She had seen the triumph on Madge's face and Simon was doing nothing to reassure her. He lengthened his stride as they crossed the street.

"What are you going to do?" she asked miserably. "Throw me in the bay?"

"Don't tempt me!" he snapped.

"Well, you could have denied it!" she said defensively.

Abruptly he stopped and turned her to face him. "Could I?" he said more quietly. "With you standing there looking like a rabbit cornered by the fox? You think I could have called you a liar and saved myself at your expense? You have a pretty odd notion of my character if you could even suggest that." He looked deeply into her eyes and read the remorse there. "Besides," he added more gently, "if I had had my way, it would have been the truth. I planted the idea in your head to begin with."

Her trembling smile thanked him for giving her a little of her self-respect back.

"Come on," he said, giving her arm a squeeze. "It's not the end of the world, but I think we'd better have a talk. In here."

The café they turned into was empty except for a couple of old-timers perched on stools at the counter. After calling out an order for two coffees to the young waitress Simon led the way to a back booth where they couldn't be overheard. He sat with his head lowered in thought until the girl had plunked down the two mugs and returned to the novel she had been reading.

"Simon," Carol began slowly, "do you really think that Madge will try to use this against you—to try and take Katie away from you?"

"Do you really doubt it?"

"No," Carol replied honestly. She had seen enough of Madge Penrod to know that nothing was beyond the woman. "What I don't understand is why! Why does Madge want Katie so badly? Oh, I know that she's her grandmother, but I could swear that she actually cares nothing at all about her! There are times when I've thought she could scarcely tolerate her."

"Do you think I don't know that?" Whatever anger he had felt had now turned to bleakness. "I love Katie dearly, but if I really thought for a moment that Madge loved her and could care for her better than I could I would let her have custody. But she doesn't and she couldn't!"

"Then why?" Carol repeated in bewilderment. "Is it just to spite you or something like that?"

"Nothing so emotionally complicated as revenge. Madge's motives are very simple and pragmatic. She's after control of Katie's fortune."

"Fortune!"

"Yes. My father died shortly after Katie was born, but before he died he set up a trust fund for her, something in the neighborhood of two million dollars. I, of course, as her legal guardian was named trustee. But if I lose custody of her and Madge assumes the guardianship she acquires complete control of both the principal and the income until Katie is twenty-one or marries—with her guardian's consent, of course. Madge doesn't want Katie, she wants the money!"

For several moments Carol could only stare at him while she digested what he was saying. Slowly she let out the breath she had taken. That explained so much! Poor Katie! Poor Simon! Oh, what harm had she done? From her own blundering stupid tongue had come the words that had placed Katie in very real jeopardy!

"I see you understand," he said simply, "and now I think it's time for you to do a little soul baring. When someone sets me up like that I want to know why. Now, what was your untimely little announcement all about?"

Carol squirmed uncomfortably as his eyes

pinned her against the cheap plastic seat of the booth. "Why—why did I say such a thing to Rick?" she stuttered, trying to buy a little time.

"Right the first time," he drawled. "Well?"

"You—you know I had been seeing a lot of Rick Sanders," she began at last. His nod urged her to continue. "Well, he had asked me to marry him and I had refused to commit myself. The night of your showing we had a fight and I told him I never wanted to see him again. He—he wasn't willing to take no for an answer."

She had been playing with the salt and pepper shakers, unable to meet Simon's eyes, and now he reached out and removed them from her limp grasp.

"So he followed you here?" he persisted.

"Yes. My aunt told him where I was. He came to take me back with him."

"And you couldn't simply have refused?"

"I lost my temper! I thought I could get rid of him once and for all if I told him . . . well, if I told him—"

"—that I was your lover," he finished for her.

"Yes!"

"Now," he said softly, "would you care to go back and fill in everything you've left out?"

His request was polite, but Carol didn't miss the command in his voice.

"I . . . I don't know what you mean!" she prevaricated.

"Has anyone ever told you that you're a lousy liar? I may be many things, but gullible isn't one of them. Now, how about the truth, the whole truth?"

Carol was no match for Simon's determination. "All right! All right!" Her hand was shaking as she lifted the cup to her lips and took a swallow.

"That night—the night of your showing—Rick had had too much to drink when he picked me up. He took me back to his apartment and when I refused to go to bed with him he was furious. Before I left he said . . . well, he said that I was frigid, that I was sexually repressed—" She stopped abruptly, unable to continue.

"So by claiming me as your lover you were telling him he was wrong, is that it?" he persisted.

"Yes!"

To her surprise a smile twitched at his lips. How could he find anything funny in the situation? she wondered indignantly.

"So Sanders thought you were sexually repressed, did he? His lack of perception doesn't surprise me."

The diner was warm and Carol had taken off her coat. The tweed jacket she wore was open. Simon's eyes were fixed on the third button of her beige silk blouse and she quickly looked down. Sometime, probably in the struggle with Rick, the button had come undone. The lace edge of her bra was just visible and a provocative amount of cleavage showed above it. A warm laugh brought her eyes back to Simon's face.

"What surprises me," he continued softly, "is that you apparently believed him!"

Right now it was surprising her, too! The look in Simon's eyes was making her heart beat wildly and the remembered touch of his hands, his lips, brought a swell of surging desire. How could she ever have believed that she was frigid?

Arthur had given her the answer and she had accepted it mentally, but not emotionally. It all seemed so clear now. She had been suffering from the repercussions of Brian's betrayal and she had not been able to see her relationship with Rick properly. She had become involved with him on the rebound and hadn't used very good judgment in her choice of a man. The problem hadn't been that she was sexually repressed. The problem had been that he was simply the wrong man!

And was Simon the right man?

Suddenly Carol felt as though the wind had been knocked out of her and she expelled a long shuddering breath. Her head was spinning, but her heart answered the unconscious question. Yes!

What had begun as a strong physical attraction for Simon had quickly escalated into sexual desire, and without her realizing it her feelings for him had developed into something much, much deeper. She was in love with Simon Forbes.

Once the admission was made it was as though a volcano had erupted inside her. She felt the hot warmth of loving and longing spread through her body. She loved Simon—wanted him, needed him!

For several moments she sat limply on the seat, sorting out the implications of this discovery. With the volatility of newly acknowledged love her spirits soared with euphoria one moment and plummeted to despair the next. She loved Simon, but she had no idea how deep his feelings for her went. Oh, he wanted her—she didn't doubt that —but on what terms and for how long?

Anxiously she chewed her bottom lip. Last night he had suggested an affair and she realized now that she had rejected the idea because she wanted more than that. When she gave herself to Simon she wanted it to be as part of a commitment, not an interlude.

She had such doubts about him! She didn't believe that he had any faith in love as she understood it. To him it was simply sexual attraction—the desire for a beautiful body. He had told her as much the night before. Did he really believe that?

Simon the artist and Simon the man. Was there a difference between them, a difference in the way they looked at a woman? She needed to know. But how? She couldn't ask without betraying her own feelings for him and she wasn't prepared to do that yet, not without some assurance that her love was returned in some measure.

She looked up and met his eyes. He was watching her with that intense scrutiny that held both warmth and appraisal at the same time, and a plan began to form in her mind. It could be dangerous. She could find herself caught in a situation beyond her control and there was no guarantee that she would discover what she wanted to know, but at the moment she was feeling desperate enough to try anything.

"I thought perhaps you had gone to sleep on me," Simon interrupted her planning. "Are you all right?"

Quickly she pressed a hand to her heated

cheek. She must look strange. She felt strange. A little wild eyed. "Simon," she said before she could change her mind, "I want you to know how much I appreciate what you did with Rick and I'm sorry I've landed you in such a mess with Madge. I wish there was something I could do—"

"Short of performing a miracle with Katie, I don't know what. A miraculous recovery is the only thing I can think of that would satisfy a judge now."

"But I want to repay you in some way," she persisted. "I owe you something—"

"You don't owe me anything, Carol."

"But I do!"

His eyes narrowed as he took in her flushed cheeks and nervous hands. "And you have something in mind?"

"Yes. I just thought—"

"Forget it!" His eyes were suddenly hard and his mouth thinned into a grim line.

"But—"

"I said forget it," he interrupted again, "if it's what I think you have in mind! I've never slept with a woman for any reason but our mutual pleasure and I don't intend to start now. I don't call in debts that way!"

Carol's face was now as pale as it had been flushed. "That wasn't what I meant," she said with quiet dignity.

"It wasn't?"

His tone wasn't encouraging, but she pressed on. "No! You did something for me that no one else could have done, against your own interests and inclinations. I want to repay you in the same way—a service."

His eyes were wary, his expression arrested. "So what exactly did you have in mind?"

Her chin tilted just a little defiantly and she met his eyes squarely. "You want me to model for you. Well, I will!"

For the space of a moment Simon sat in stunned silence. He had obviously not expected this. Then, "You agree to model for me?"

"Yes."

"Er . . . unconditionally?"

"If by that," she said dryly, "you mean will I take off my clothes and let down my hair, the answer is yes."

A sudden smile broke over his face. "Defeat, Carol?"

"Not at all," she said coolly. "I'm offering you my services as—as recompense. Do you accept?"

The hand that covered hers on the table was warm and intimate. "I'd be a fool not to."

Chapter Eight

The next day, after Carol had finished her morning session with Katie, she returned to her room to find Simon waiting. He had on his work clothes and the spatterings of clay told her that he had indeed been working.

"Did you mean what you said yesterday?" he asked abruptly.

"About modeling for you?" she asked, knowing full well that that was what he meant.

She had had a great many qualms during the whole restless night and Simon's appearance now did nothing to alleviate them. He was so . . . so essentially *male* in those tight-fitting jeans slung low on his hips and molded to his powerful thighs. His head was tossed a little arrogantly to one side as he looked at her. His thumbs were stuck in the back pockets of his pants as he slouched nonchalantly against the wall, but she sensed his excitement. She almost told him no—until she saw that familiar gleam in his eyes. The *artist* gleam.

Could a man who cared about a woman at all look at her and see only her outward form? Artist or not, if he felt anything at all for the woman inside the body, could he so easily detach himself from what made her a person?

"If you've changed your mind . . ." he said into the silence.

"No!"

"You know I wouldn't force you, Carol."

She swallowed the lump of tension in her throat. Now was not the time to get cold feet. "No," she repeated firmly. "I'm willing."

"I told you that I don't mix business with pleasure," he reminded her unnecessarily.

"I know what you told me," she said, trying to keep the bitterness out of her voice.

He frowned as he caught something behind her words that he didn't understand. "You don't believe me?"

The problem was, she was afraid she did!

How ironic, she concluded. In the beginning Simon had been afraid of her profession. He had been afraid that Carol the psychologist would see too much of what lay beneath the surface persona he presented to the world. Now *she* was afraid of *his* profession, afraid that Simon the artist would see too little!

"Oh, for heaven's sake," she said impatiently, stirred by these misgivings. "I offered to model, didn't I?"

"I know," he said curtly, responding to her mood, "but something is eating you."

He was certainly perceptive about *some* things! she concluded miserably. At least she was sure he had no idea how she felt about him.

He waited a moment for her reply, but when she stood straight and uncommunicative, he shrugged. "All right. We'll start after lunch. Is Katie joining us?"

"We've set the pattern of having her at meals. I think we ought to continue. The more she sees of you, the better."

Her judgment was verified. Ada had been taken with a cold, so only the three of them sat down to eat. Katie had reverted to her slacks and a sweater and the hated doll was now conspicuous by its absence. If possible, she had been more relieved than the adults in the household by the departure of her grandmother.

As she took her place at the table she shot her father a quick glance—a nervous glance, but not fearful. Then she thoughtfully looked back and forth between Carol and Simon, and a smile of satisfaction curved her lips. It was almost as though she had said: just the three of us. A family. How nice.

Carol caught and interpreted the look and she felt a tug in the region of her heart. This was the first time that Katie had actually looked like a happy, normal child.

Oh, dear! she thought as she returned Katie's smile. I not only love Simon, I'm afraid that I love his daughter as well. She knew that she was letting herself in for a lot of heartache when she finally had to leave the little family.

Perhaps she wouldn't have to leave, a hopeful part of her mind suggested. If Simon could come to love her. . . . Don't set yourself up for disappointment, her rational self responded severely. Only time would tell.

As lunch progressed Simon began to sense the difference in his daughter's attitude. She was eating well and no longer jumped when he spoke to her. By the end of the meal he was watching her covertly, a thoughtful expression in his eyes, and when Amy arrived to take her out to play he stood. Almost involuntarily his hand went out to Katie. A tense silence kept the three adults motionless as they waited for her reaction.

Slowly the child raised her eyes to Carol's and almost imperceptibly Carol nodded. Like a quivering bird, the girl's hand met her father's. By degrees he tightened his fingers, giving her every opportunity to pull away if she chose. She didn't.

Simon had the good sense not to ask for more than this brief overture. "Have a good day, Katie," he said casually, and the reward for his patience was a small shy smile.

As Katie left the room with Amy, Carol met Simon's eyes and caught the suspicion of a tear there. They both knew that a minor miracle had occurred.

"Are you ready?" he asked a half hour later when they met in the hall. "You'll need your coat."

"Where are we going?" she returned in some surprise. She had never been in Simon's studio, but she had assumed that it was somewhere in the upper reaches of the house in the wing opposite her own. She had been curious, of course, but had respected Simon's need for privacy while he worked and had never tried to investigate.

"I wondered if you would ever ask. You've shown a remarkable lack of curiosity about my retreat."

"Where is it?"

"Do you know why Bar Harbor happened to grow the way it did?" he asked in reply, helping her into her leather coat.

"Not really."

"Just after the turn of the century the wealthy of Boston, New York and Philadelphia society turned it into a summer playground. The result was the modest little mansions that dot the area. My family chose to build here on Porcupine Island. It had been in our family for over a century."

"Just a short hop from Philadelphia, of course," she drawled.

Simon grinned. "Far enough away for people to forget that the original Forbes who discovered the place was a pirate who grew too old to pillage and became a respectable shipper."

And the legacy he had left Simon was more than the fortune he had acquired, she thought, remembering her first impression of him in Bar Harbor. She had recognized that pirate blood!

"Did he build the castle?"

"No. My grandfather built it in 1906. It took nearly two years to haul in the New Hampshire granite for it."

She could believe it, she thought as they passed through the front door and down the broad granite steps. The November wind whipped against her face and blew the light snow into little whirling circles as Simon guided her down a path that led into the pine forest to the right of the house.

"Simon, where are we going?"

"Well, one of the little games the idle rich liked to play was 'roughing it.'"

"Huh!" she sniffed, glancing back at the castle rising majestically behind them.

"Exactly. So people like my grandfather built cabins out in the woods within easy reach of all the comforts of home, but far enough out of sight to create the illusion of the old pioneer spirit. They would come out and spend a day or two—hauling water from the stream and chopping wood for the stove."

Now Carol understood. "And you've turned the cabin into your studio."

"With a few minor alterations. I needed more natural light. You'll see in a minute, as soon as we're clear of these trees."

They had descended a hollow, crossed a log bridge spanning a now frozen stream and were climbing the hill on the other side. A moment later Carol had her first glimpse of Simon's hideaway; it could hardly be called a cabin. The log structure was large. A chimney rose at one end.

The roof on the other side slanted oddly, somewhat awkwardly. This must have been Simon's addition, she concluded.

Simon's hand on her arm was firm as he helped her over a fallen log. As she glanced around her she was suddenly struck with the thought that they would be very isolated out here in the studio. They had left all traces of civilization behind them and were surrounded now by nothing but trees, leafless shrubs and decaying ferns. What would she do if Simon broke his own rules and suddenly decided to mix business with pleasure? Would that be enough to give her the answers she wanted?

Probably not, she concluded morosely. He had never denied that physical beauty stirred physical need. But what else did it stir? That was the question.

Simon stood aside to allow her to precede him into the converted studio. At one time the cabin had obviously been divided into separate rooms, but Simon had had the walls knocked out to create one large space, rising up to the rafters above. The heat that filtered through the room came from a large Franklin stove at one end.

For the first few minutes Carol almost forgot Simon's presence as she looked around the room in fascination. The tile on the floor was spattered with clay and strewn with various pieces of debris —wood, wire, pipe, large empty buckets. A nearly finished piece of sculpture to one side was covered with damp cloths. On the other side an odd contraption of wood, twisted wire and bent lead pipe stood some eight feet in height on a metal base. Large buckets filled with clay took up one entire long shelf.

The pieces of furniture that adorned the room were an odd collection of chairs, stools, worktables and a daybed that had been pushed against the wall. The oversized sink in a kitchen area was far more functional than attractive. Two shaded lights hung down into the room, but other lights set in the ceiling gave off an indirect glow that approximated natural light and supplemented the slanting skylight.

"Well, what do you think of it?" Simon asked, breaking the silence.

"It's fascinating," she answered honestly.

"I'm glad you think so," he said. "You're going to have plenty of time to enjoy it."

His comment brought her thoughts back to her purpose there with a jolt. Her attention had been so centered on the place itself that she had nearly forgotten why she had come.

"You can hang your coat here on one of the hooks," he said, removing his own sheepskin jacket. "I'll put more wood on the fire and turn on the space heaters. I wouldn't want you to catch cold."

He spoke so nonchalantly that Carol almost missed the import of his words. He didn't want her to catch cold! With her clothes off!

"Simon . . ." she began.

"Let's get started while the light is good," he said, ignoring the sudden panic in her tone and crossing to the shelves for his sketch pad and box of charcoal.

"Simon . . ." she tried again.

"Yes?"

He turned on her suddenly, pinning her under his gaze, and the words died in her throat. This had been her choice and there was no going back.

"What—what do you want me to do?" she gulped.

His expression softened a little as he accurately read the anxiety in her face. "I'm not a monster, you know," he chided. "I'm an artist. And you are a very beautiful woman. I knew what I wanted to create that night in your room."

"Wh-what?"

He hesitated a moment and then indicated two easy chairs in front of the stove. "Sit down. I'm going to get us some wine. We'll relax here for a while and I'll explain what I have in mind." A rueful smile curved his lips. "Heroic martyrdom isn't exactly the expression I want on your face— for Joan of Arc, perhaps, but not Beatrice."

"Beatrice?" she asked, her interest aroused.

"As in Dante and Beatrice." He had opened a small refrigerator under the counter and taken out a bottle of white wine. While he poured out the two glasses Carol sank into a chair.

"Here," he said, handing her one. "But take your time with it. I want you relaxed, not sloshed." An old wooden chair groaned under his weight as he joined her. "You've read the *Divine Comedy?*"

"Years ago, in college, but I don't remember much about it," she admitted. "Who exactly was Beatrice?"

"The fiction Dante created was far more romantic than the actual fact, I'm afraid." His smile turned cynical. "But isn't that true of most romances? The expectation, the anticipation and the fantasy seldom equal the reality." She knew he was thinking of Angela. "That's why an affair is so much more satisfactory than marriage. When disillusionment sets in the tie can be quickly and painlessly broken."

Carol winced at the cynicism of his words. She wanted to blurt out a contradiction, but restrained herself. She was beginning to fear that this experiment was going to work too well. She was discovering aspects of Simon's feelings that were very discouraging.

"So Beatrice was . . . ?" she prompted, not wanting to dwell on this pessimistic speculation.

"In his writing, Beatrice was his love. Two years after her death he began writing his great poetic tribute to her in *La Vita Nuova—The New Life*. In the *Divine Comedy* he deified her, made her the goddess who conducted the poet from purgatory through paradise."

"I think that's beautiful!" Carol whispered, caught up in the romance of such a great love immortalized.

"As I said, the reality was far less romantic. Beatrice lived on an estate near Dante's and the only time he ever saw her was when she was eight and he was nine. There was no affair. They each married another, but her death three years after her marriage apparently stirred him. It's his romantic ideal that I want to capture."

Carol didn't know whether it was the effect of the wine or Simon's matter-of-fact approach to the subject that was gradually loosening her taut muscles and easing her nervous tension.

"You admire Dante, don't you?"

"Yes. Very much. I think I understand him. Dante was a Florentine and I spent two of the happiest years of my life studying in Florence."

Those were the two years just before his marriage, Carol remembered. What must he have been like then? Nearly ten years younger. Idealistic? Optimistic? Oh, she would have loved to have known him then!

"You—you told me that I have a quality you wanted to capture," she said diffidently. "What? I can't imagine that I'm anything like Beatrice."

He gave her his long assessing regard. "No, certainly not in coloring. Beatrice would undoubtedly have been dark, but in bronze that makes no difference."

"Then what?"

"Your cool reserve. Your lack of awareness of your physical beauty. Your air of innocence that's enough to drive a man wild. You invite seduction without even knowing it with your subtle sensuality."

His analytic tone robbed the words of the personal. He might just as well have been describing a vase of flowers.

Simon saw her frown and misinterpreted it. "You don't believe me?" he asked. "But, then, you don't see yourself as a man does. You don't see yourself walk or sit or stand. You don't know that when you look at me you tilt your head just a little to one side and watch me out of the corner of your eyes. Very sexy! And have you any idea at all how you respond to a man?"

Not any man, she wanted to cry. You, Simon! You!

"Are you ready?" he said abruptly. Apparently the time for talking had ended. "Today all I want to do is make the first preliminary sketches."

"You mean draw?"

"Yes. That's the way I work. We'll try several different poses until I find the one that's best. Then, each time you come for a sitting, we'll reproduce that pose with the aid of the sketch and begin working in clay. I have the name for the statue already: *Quest for Paradise*. Beatrice leading Dante from purgatory into paradise. I think it's plenty warm in here now. You can take off your clothes."

Nervously she looked around for a place to go. The bathroom was nothing but a semipartitioned corner of the room. Her options were to close herself into the metal shower stall—which she knew would afford Simon a great deal of amusement—or brazen it out. She decided on the latter as the most dignified course. The question was, where to begin?

Shoes and socks seemed safest. Still sitting, she slipped off her loafers, pulled up the legs of her jeans and rolled down her socks. She had to stand to remove the rest of her clothing and she schooled her mind to blankness, using all her willpower to block out the image of Simon sitting quietly, intently watching her.

She pulled her sweater over her head and slowly began the process of unbuttoning her blouse. Her fingers fumbled with the buttons until the procedure was a torture. Once they were undone, she removed the garment with a quick careless gesture, afraid to let him know how erotic she found the experience. Her bra followed and she stood topless before him, her breasts high, firm and beautifully rounded, the nipples hard with unwanted arousal.

For just a moment she paused at the waist of her jeans.

"Everything, Carol," Simon ordered quietly.

Their eyes met and what she saw in his cooled her heated blood and renewed her determination to continue. His gaze was warm but thoughtful, as though he were measuring her figure in strictly mathematical terms of symmetry and proportion. Well, she could match him for disinterest! Detached, calm, stoic and unblushing, that was her.

After the last of her clothing dropped to the floor a moment of silence stretched out to what seemed an eternity. Finally Simon spoke.

"You're even more beautiful than I dreamed!"

"From such a connoisseur I have to take that as a compliment," she said with forced lightness.

"Definitely. But you've forgotten something."

Forgotten what? she wondered wildly, stifling the impulse to giggle. Not an inch of her was covered by so much as a layer of fingernail polish!

"Your hair," he reminded gently. "Turn around and let it down."

Gratefully she turned her back to him and raised her hands to the chignon at the nape of the neck. One by one she removed the oversized tortoiseshell hairpins that she had used to hold it in place. Carelessly she tossed them on a nearby table and with a shake of her head sent the thick roll of hair cascading down her back to the base of her spine. She jumped as she felt Simon's hands loosening and separating the heavy strands until they formed a waterfall over her bare back. She didn't turn to face him again, but she felt him withdraw. In a moment, however, he was back.

"Put this on."

She turned her head to look over her shoulder at him. He held a thin robe of white silk.

Thankfully she slipped her arms into the sleeves, but her relief was short-lived as she saw that the robe did little to conceal her nude body. The sleeves were long and wide, but they were cut from the hemmed wrists to the shoulder seams so that her arms were free and the fabric hung in drapes down her sides. The lapels of the open front widened at the shoulders to form the cowl that rested on her back.

Carefully Simon pulled her long hair free from the collar, turned her and arranged the front lapels so that her breasts were bare and the robe became little more than a sliver of silk shimmering down her body. The back of his hand touched her heated flesh as he rearranged a drape here, a fold there, and by the time he had finished the eyes she turned toward him were glazed, the muscles of her face strained.

"Relax," he ordered curtly, reproof in his voice.

"I can't!" she gasped.

"Yes, you can. We'll talk of other things. Now, do you see the wood and metal frame?" he asked, pointing to the odd contraption Carol had noted before. "Well, that's the armature on which I'll build the sculpture in clay. The pipe is flexible so I can bend it to conform to the pose I choose. Now, turn your body slightly, look back over your shoulder and extend your hand in a beckoning gesture. . . . Yes, that's it. Now just hold that for a few minutes. Tell me if you get too tired."

Once again his matter-of-factness had slowed her racing pulse. He perched on a stool, the charcoal on a nearby table and the sketch pad on his knee.

"When did you know you wanted to be a sculptor, Simon?" When did you start seeing women as art objects? was what she really wanted to ask.

"Do you know, I can hardly remember a time when I wasn't pushing and poking and kneading clay. I must have been about nine when I discovered a little deposit of clay where a tree had been uprooted. The quality wasn't the greatest, but it was good enough for me. In my teens, when I was home from school during the summers, I used to con Ada and even Sam into modeling for me. I loved their faces."

"You grew up with them?" He was right, she thought. Talking of other things *was* helping her relax.

"Oh, Ada's connection with my family goes back a long way. My mother died when I was very young and Ada came here to live as my father's— how shall I say?—very close friend. As you have probably guessed, she was an actress in her prime—small-time and not always respectable, but she was like a second mother to me. . . . Tip your chin up just slightly. That's good."

"And Sam?" she persisted.

"A beachcomber, scavenger, whatever you want to call it. But he had a way with anything mechanical and my father offered him a job working on the island."

"You have an unusual household. I almost don't dare ask. Amy and Arnold?"

"I acquired them only recently—out of a juvenile detention home. They're the third pair I've had. The others have rejoined the world, I hope as useful members of society."

"The cook? Let me guess! A bag woman from New York?"

"Don't laugh!" he chided. "You moved your head. Bring your chin back down."

"Yes, sir," she murmured contritely. For a moment she had forgotten what she was doing and was simply enjoying the conversation.

"Nell," he continued when she resumed the proper pose, "was a Bar Harbor native who couldn't face the nursing home where her children were going to have her put away."

With her head tilted the way it was Carol couldn't see his face well, but she heard the compassion in his voice. "You really care about them all, don't you, Simon?"

"Yes, I care. Except for Katie, they're all the family I have."

Oh, Simon, let me be part of that family! her heart cried longingly.

"Now you can relax for a minute," he was saying, obviously unaware of her inner turmoil.

He stood and stretched, and Carol could not help but note his lithe grace. His muscles seemed to move in perfect rhythm and coordination. He would be a wonderful lover. . . . Stop it! she ordered herself.

He was beside her again, his head tilted, viewing her from a different angle. She almost flinched when he put out his hand to gather her hair over one shoulder.

"This time I want to draw you from the back. Keep your head straight ahead."

A moment later he was back on his stool and Carol felt far less self-conscious in this pose.

"Simon?" she began hesitantly. "How did you happen to specialize in . . . well, in erotic art?"

"I prefer to call it romantic art, though both terms are appropriate—the one just had more commercial appeal."

"So, why did you choose it?"

"I have my stay in Italy to thank. Romance—the search or quest for the erotic, man-woman love—helped usher in the Renaissance."

"How?"

"Oh, in the Middle Ages man sought God through the authoritarian church. Then along came humanistic philosophy. Humanism—the importance of the individual—stimulated another kind of thought. Man began looking for God in other human beings. One of the great obsessions became the quest for romance." He paused. "Turn your chin just a little toward me."

Obediently she did as he asked and he studied

her a moment in silence. Then, "Do you know what paradise means?"

"Well, heaven, I guess."

"Yes, heaven—the final resting place for worthy souls. But in its broader sense it means a place of ideal happiness. Man searches for that ideal in a woman. Dante sought it in Beatrice. That's what I am trying to capture in this work."

He made it all sound so practical, so logical—so abstract!

"Relax, Carol," he said sharply. "You've gone all stiff on me!"

The sharpness in his voice hurt almost as much as the admission that it looked as though all her fears about Simon had been realized. She wasn't sure she understood everything he had said, but one point was clear. He looked at romance strictly as an extension of an artistic perspective. Romance was for him physical beauty, a perfection of shape and form, the harmonious organization of parts. Simon admired her—and, yes, desired her—because she had an aesthetically pleasing body. He had no interest at all in what she thought or felt, no interest in the soul beneath the blond hair and smooth skin.

No, Simon didn't see her as a thinking, feeling woman at all.

Chapter Nine

One-thirty. Carol had half an hour before she was to meet Simon in the studio. Time enough to change her clothes, say good-bye to Katie and make the quarter-mile trek. As she had done now for the past four days, she stripped off her jeans and the remainder of her clothing. After the first afternoon she had decided to avoid a repetition of the slow disrobing process that did nothing but unsettle her. Now it was simply a matter of untying the belt to her denim wraparound, pulling off her boots and stockings and slipping into the white silk robe.

Simon's smile had been knowing that second day, but ultimately, she concluded a little bitterly, he was as relieved as she not to have the unveiling belabored.

The only moment Simon the man had shown through had occurred on the third day, when he was adjusting her arm to put it in exactly the right position. Inadvertently his hand had brushed against the hard peak of her breast. For a fraction of a minute he had paused as he felt her heated pulsing response. She sighed in irritation as she remembered the hot surging longing that had coursed through her body. From then on he had been very careful to see that he didn't touch her again.

Not bothering to check her appearance in the mirror, Carol went quickly out into the hall and along the corridor to the playroom. Katie was certainly happier these days and more relaxed, but Carol could still find no clue to the problem that kept her silent.

The door to the playroom was open and Amy sat crosswise in the large overstuffed chair, her legs across the arms as she read a book and munched on an apple. Katie sat in the middle of the room on the large hooked rug. On her lap was the doll that her grandmother had given her. Carol paused just outside the door. Was it going to happen again?

As soon as the girl had found that her grandmother had gone for good she had thrown the doll into a corner in an untidy heap. There it had remained for two days. Then, a few days ago, Katie had retrieved it. For a long time she had simply stared at it. Then, to Carol's surprise, she had taken it by one arm and shaken it. Sitting down, she bent it across her knee and began to spank it, gently at first and then with an increasing violence.

Carol had watched the girl's face with amazement. The expressions that flitted across the small features ran the gamut from fear to anger and finally to sorrow. What had motivated such an outburst, and who did the doll represent?

As Carol watched the ritual began again. First the shaking and then the pounding and, as before, at the end, Katie took the doll by one leg and threw it in the corner, her eyes bleak and haunted.

"Katie," Carol said with forced cheerfulness as she entered the room, "I just came to say goodbye, sweetheart. I'm on my way to the studio. I'll see you at dinner."

It took Katie's eyes a moment to leave the inner vision that held her and focus on Carol. Then with a cry she ran and flung her arms around her.

"Have a good afternoon," Carol murmured fondly, kissing the upturned face. "Bundle up well if you go outside. It's been snowing for the past hour."

"Bundle up, Carol," Ada echoed a few minutes later as Carol tied the leather belt to her coat and pulled a knit hat down over her head. "Sam radioed in a few minutes ago. He and Simon have been putting the boat away. Gale warnings are out. Looks like it might be blowing up the first nor'easter of the season."

The storm was picking up in intensity, Carol noted as she headed for the woods. The sky was almost as dark as night and the wind whipped around her bare legs. She was panting from exertion by the time she climbed the final hill to the isolated studio. The trees had offered some protection, but even so she had been walking against the wind and nearly four inches of heavy wet snow had accumulated on the path. Thankfully she opened the door and a sudden strong gust of wind propelled her into the room. She had to lean her shoulder against the heavy pine door to get it closed again.

The room was in darkness and she fumbled for the light switch. Was she early? She checked her watch. No, ten after two. She was late, but so was Simon. She shivered. At first the room had felt warm after the biting cold outside, but now that her body was adjusting she knew that actually it couldn't be much over forty degrees inside. She could see her breath. The electric space heaters were turned off and the fire in the stove had gone out. Well, that gave her something to do until Simon arrived.

After turning on the heaters and building the fire she checked her watch again. Going on three. Odd. Where was Simon? Delayed down at the boat harbor, probably, she thought with a shrug.

The fire was burning brightly and after adding a few lumps of coal she settled down in the easy chair to wait. It was really very cozy. She yawned and stretched, her thoughts clouding. She hadn't been sleeping well and the exertion of the hike coupled with the lazy warmth of the fire was making her drowsy. Taking off her boots, she settled herself deeper into the soft cushions and cuddled under the mohair lap robe. Simon ought to be there any minute, she thought as her eyes slowly began to close. She would just rest. . . .

Five minutes later she was fast asleep. The crackle of the shortwave radio in the corner became a part of her dreams. She was in a cave, walking on cellophane. From somewhere in the depths of the cave Simon was calling her, but his voice was muffled and very far away.

"Carol! Carol! Come in, please! Over!"

Over what? Over where? The cellophane crackled underfoot.

"Can you hear me? Are you there? Over!"

Of course I'm here. You don't need to shout, Simon. . . .

The darkness of the storm had given way to the darkness of the night before Carol awakened, shivering under the mohair robe. There was no light in the room and the fire was only a glow. Memory returned with a rush. Where was Simon? She checked the lighted digits on her watch. Six o'clock! She must have been asleep for nearly three hours!

Vaguely she looked around the room, trying to banish the last remnants of sleep. The lights were out and the heaters had been turned off. Simon must have been there. Why hadn't he wakened her?

She shivered again and tried to straighten her legs. She was stiff with the cold. Tentatively she stood, holding on to the chair for support as the pins and needles shot through her legs. Oww!

The first thing was to build the fire back up. She

could still hear the wind whistling around the house. Rather than abating, the storm seemed to have increased in intensity. Quickly she pushed more paper into the grate, where the heat from the coals sent it into instant life. She got kindling from the woodbox and finally more logs. Once this was done to her satisfaction she put on her boots, scurried across to the door and flicked the light switch. Nothing! She flipped it again. Still nothing. Slowly she realized that Simon had never come. He hadn't turned off the lights. The lines must have gone down in the storm!

For a moment she panicked, then realized the stupidity of worrying. So what if she didn't have any electricity? She would take a few minutes to get warm and gather her wits and then she would go back to the house. Could she see the lights of the castle from the window?

The sight that met her eyes was far from encouraging. The outside world was nothing but a blur of dark, whirling flakes. She couldn't even see the trees on the edge of the clearing! She would be a fool to leave the relative security of the studio for the blizzard outside.

Don't panic! she counseled herself as she let out a breath and realized she could once again see the vapor in the freezing air of the room. Quickly she returned to the stove and breathed an unconscious sigh of relief that her fire was taking hold. She had plenty of wood and an ample supply of coal to see her through any emergency. So what if she had to stay the night? She could at least stay warm.

For several moments more she contemplated what was best to do to make herself comfortable. Were there any candles around? Did Simon keep any food?

In a drawer underneath the counter she discovered a whole box of stubby utilitarian candles and a book of matches. Quickly she lighted two of the candles and propped them up in a shallow jar. The refrigerator yielded only half a bottle of wine, a quart of milk, a little cheese and an apple. Meager fare, but she wouldn't starve. Her foray into the cupboards was more productive. A box of soda crackers, a can of baked beans, a canned ham and several jars of home-preserved fruit. Now, here was a feast!

Her nose was nearing the frostbite stage when she discovered the kerosene lanterns. In a moment she had the two lamps burning, casting a warm, pleasant glow around her. Carefully she carried them back to the little oasis of warmth around the stove and set them on the table beside her chair. She wasn't hungry yet and would wait a little while to eat. Perhaps that would help pass what threatened to be a very long, lonely night. Heroically she stifled the wish that Simon were there to share the long hours with her.

What time was it now? Only seven. What were they doing at the castle? she wondered idly, wrapping the mohair robe around her and settling into the chair. Had the electricity gone out there also? Were Ada, Simon and Katie sitting down to dinner—

A sudden crash brought her to her feet. The

front door had flown open and banged into the wall. Wind and snow blew six feet into the room and there, clutching at the door frame, stood Simon! His heavy sheepskin jacket was covered with snow. A layer of white covered the hat pulled down low on his face. Beads of ice had formed on his eyebrows and around the rim of the wool cap. He looked like a wild man—half-frozen and raging with anger.

He paused only a moment while he caught his breath and then he pulled at the door and slammed it into place. When he turned back to her Carol saw that he was shaking.

"Simon! Are you all right?"

"Am I all right!" he roared. "My God! You ask me that?"

"What's the matter?" she asked in bewilderment.

"The matter!"

She stamped her foot in frustration. "Simon, will you stop repeating everything I say and answer me? What's wrong?"

In one swift movement he lunged across the room toward her, his gait unsteady, as though his legs could hardly support him. Before he reached her he tore the hat from his head, slapped off his ice-encrusted gloves and dumped his coat on the floor. Frenziedly he plucked her out from behind the footstool and dragged her against his chest. His trembling hands moved up and down her back and over her arms as if to reassure himself that she was indeed flesh and blood and not some figment of his fevered imagination.

Carol was convinced now that he was ill. His eyes were unnaturally bright and his body trembled against hers.

"My God!" he groaned. "I thought you were dead!"

"Dead?" Carol's voice was muffled against his thick sweater.

With shaking hands he pushed her away from him and stared down into her face, drinking in the sight of her wide eyes and parted lips. With a moan he pulled her hard against him once again and took those lips in a kiss that threatened to devour her. She felt weightless as he scooped her up into his arms and collapsed with her into the chair, his mouth never leaving hers.

It was several moments before he even gave her a chance to breathe and she was panting when he finally buried his face in her neck and expelled a great shuddering sigh.

"I thought you were dead," he repeated huskily.

"Why?" she murmured, her body still trembling in reaction to his sudden onslaught. "What's wrong?"

Slowly he eased his hold a fraction of an inch. "Why in heaven's name didn't you answer the radio?"

"Radio? What radio?"

"I called for one solid hour, and then Sam and I began the search. I had nearly given up hope when I saw the light through the window!"

"You—you've been out in the storm looking for me?" she gasped, pulling back to look up into his face. "But why? Ada knew I was here."

"That's what I tried to explain! This is where we both thought you were, but you didn't answer the radio call! I came down myself periodically, but the house was dark."

"The electricity went out and I was asleep in the chair," she said weakly, still dazed by the realization that Simon must have been out for two or three hours hunting for her in that awful blizzard. "Oh, Simon!"

With a shudder she burrowed against him, trying to give him some of her warmth. Oh, if anything had happened to him she would have wanted to die! At that moment her love for him was overwhelming. She wanted to take him right into herself, to share her love and life and longing. He was so cold. His cheek on hers was like ice.

He felt the shudder that trembled through her and raised her head with a hand under her chin, his eyes anxiously searching her face. "Are you sure you're all right?"

"Yes! It's you I'm worried about!" Reluctantly she disengaged herself from his arms. "Sit here and let me get you something to drink. Do you keep anything stronger than wine around?"

His hands lingered on her hips as she stood. "There's a bottle of bourbon in the cupboard above the hot plate."

"I'm afraid you're going to have to take it straight," she said with a lightness she didn't feel. The white lines around his mouth worried her. "I think the pipes are frozen."

"Straight is fine." He gratefully accepted the glass half-filled with whiskey. Before he realized her intention she had knelt in front of him, unzipped his heavy boots and begun easing them from his feet.

"What are you doing?" he protested.

"Just be quiet and drink your bourbon," she scolded.

At least he had dressed properly, she thought as he settled back into the chair. He was wearing three heavy pairs of socks under the fur-lined waterproof boots. Even so, his feet were frozen, and for several minutes she chafed them gently.

"Simon," she asked at last, "do you have any extra clothes here? Your pants are soaking wet."

"No, I change at the house." His words were slightly slurred. The combination of warmth and whiskey was working quickly. She couldn't allow him to fall into a false contentment until she had him dry.

"Well, then," she said firmly, "you're just going to have to wrap up in a blanket! Now, stand up and take your pants off."

Only one eye opened to stare at her.

"Come on! Up you get!" she prodded. "You get your pants off and I'll get a blanket from the bed."

A slow smile of amusement spread over his face, easing the lines of tension. "Ah! I see! Positions are reversed. Now it's *you* who watch *me* undress!"

"What's the matter?" she asked pertly, suppressing the impulse to blush. "Shy? A little taste of your own medicine?"

"You're mighty brave all of a sudden, love," he drawled.

There was delicious danger in what she was doing, Carol knew, but suddenly it no longer seemed to matter. She had been too shaken at the thought of losing him. She loved him and at this moment nothing else was important.

"Take your pants off, Simon. Please! You've got to get warm!"

"You know, I've never been begged more nicely. I'm feeling warmer and warmer by the minute!"

Carol believed him. The color had returned to his face and his eyes had lost that fevered glaze. The look he gave her now was very much alive and alight with a different kind of excitement.

Slowly he levered himself out of the chair until he towered over her where she sat on the hearth. Her breath caught in her throat as she watched his hands fumble with the zipper on his cords. A small gasp escaped her lips before she realized that underneath he wore a second pair of pants, skintight old jeans. The cords came off first; then he pulled down the zipper on the jeans.

"A little like the dance of the seven veils, isn't it?" he teased. His keen eyes hadn't missed her wide-eyed interest.

"You—you could have been a model yourself," she said breathlessly, resisting the impulse to reach out and stroke those strong, firm, hairy legs.

"You won't be surprised, then, to learn that I did a little modeling in art school. I was thought to have a very nice backside," he offered provocatively.

He had hooked his thumbs into the elastic waist

of his undershorts, and Carol had had all she could take of this teasing, tantalizing process. Simon knew exactly what he was doing to her!

"I'll get the blanket," she said quickly, crossing to the bed.

"Oh, but then you'll miss my big finale!"

"Stop it, Simon!" she pleaded weakly. Her resistance to him was nil!

A tender smile curved his lips and he took pity on her. By the time she had returned with the blanket he had the lap robe wrapped around his hips.

"Are—are you hungry?" she asked.

"Yes, I'm hungry!" Their eyes met and she knew just what it was he hungered for. "But first I have to radio the house and tell them to call off the search."

"I—I'm so sorry about what happened, Simon," she said faintly. She was finding it difficult to breathe.

"Well, it wasn't really your fault. By the time I called Ada from the boat dock to tell you to stay put, you had already left. She sent Arnold out to stop you, but he fell and sprained his ankle and had to limp back. Panic didn't set in until after I returned and tried to get you on the radio."

"Oh, Simon!" She shuddered again at the thought of what might have happened to him.

"Don't look like that, Carol," he said gently, resting his palm against her cheek. "I'm beginning to think that this has turned out just fine after all."

"You—you got through to Ada all right?" she asked a few moments later. Her heart was now pounding painfully against the thin layer of her dress. "What did you tell her?"

"That you were with me and that we wouldn't come back until it was safe."

"When will that be?"

His eyes locked on hers and she felt a tingle of anticipation dance up and down her spine. Here they were—alone and isolated—with one stove to keep them warm, two lanterns for light and one narrow bed to sleep in!

"Tomorrow, the next day—or when we feel like it," he said softly. "You're not modeling for me now, Carol. This is just pleasure!"

Slowly he closed the distance between them, his eyes never leaving her face.

"Do you know what I thought that first day here in the studio when you stood there in your white robe looking so indescribably lovely?"

"Wh-what?"

"I thought of a poem by Dante I learned years ago in Florence. Roughly translated, it ends with:

"If you find a man, a lover of beauty,
And he asks you to reveal yourself to him,
Show your body and
Let it be desired in love."

The deep, husky swell of his voice as he spoke the love poem made her tremble with overpowering longing. "Desired in love?" she questioned faintly.

"The quest for paradise. The place of ideal happiness, only to be found on this earth with another person. Sexual ecstasy. The artist in my eye and heart loves and appreciates your exquisite loveliness. The man in me wants to possess that beauty!"

His words set her on fire. She no longer knew nor cared what kind of love it was that he offered her. She loved him desperately—wanted him, needed him with a desire that equaled his own. She could no longer fight him and herself.

Slowly she pulled at the tie holding her dress in place. Simon's eyes never left hers as she shrugged the simple denim off her shoulders and down her arms to let it fall in a heap around her feet. She did not turn from him as she raised her hands to her hair and freed it from its pins.

"Desire me in love, Simon," she said quietly, solemnly.

"Never doubt that I do, my love!"

His hands moved and the mohair robe fell free from around his hips. Off came the sweater he wore. Then he undid the buttons down the front of his flannel shirt and let it join the growing pile of clothes at their feet. In another moment they stood there together, the leaping flames turning their bodies golden.

The muscles rippled in his arms as he reached out to hold her. He was infinitely gentle, infinitely tender as he drew her closer and closer into his embrace. His lips began their subtle exploration almost reverently at first and then with a growing passion as their bodies moved against each other in the rhythmic search for fulfillment. As his tongue circled her lips and then penetrated her mouth she grew too weak to stand and only Simon's strength supported her.

Slowly he lowered her to the floor in front of the fire. Their clothes became their pillow, the soft robe their bed. At last she knew the pleasure of total surrender to his wonderful hands as he caressed her warm flesh. Every touch scorched like fire until her entire body was aflame with desire for him.

She could not keep her own hands still. Her fingers sought out the soft mat of hair on his chest, followed the growth down to his hard flat stomach and then up to the smoothness of his shoulders. She could feel the muscles working like steel cables in his arms.

Oh, she thought dizzily as she entwined her fingers in his thick dark hair, Simon was right! The human body was beautiful!

He moved and she felt his hard, urgent passion. Neither of them would be able to endure this subtle, exquisite, torturous delay for long. Their need for each other was too great. When he followed each caress of his hands with the searing touch of his lips Carol was the first to break under the strain.

"Simon!" she cried in need and frustration. "Simon, please!"

"I know, my love. I know!"

She gasped as he moved to lie over her and the hot, hard strength of him pressed against her. Her breath was caught in trembling expectation. For just a moment he paused, his body arched above her as he looked down into her face.

"You may not be Beatrice, my darling," he murmured, "but you have brought me to the gates of paradise!"

Chapter Ten

During the night the temperature outside had dropped to near zero. The fire in the stove became only a warm glow. Crystals of ice had formed on the insides of the windowpanes to catch the first rays of the morning sun. Carol, however, had not noticed the cold. She slept soundly, nestled in a cocoon of wonderful, beautiful warmth.

As the sun rose and light filled the studio Carol turned, half-asleep, half-awake, and felt the weight of a hand slide from her back over her arm to her left breast, where it came to rest in unconscious possession.

"Mmmm," she murmured, snuggling back against Simon's warm body behind her.

"Mmmm," came an answering murmur of contentment in her ear, and the masculine leg that rode easily between her own settled itself higher.

She had just started to sink once more into sleep when she felt the hand on her breast begin a teasing caress. She turned her head to look into Simon's face so near her own. His eyes were closed, his lips slightly parted, his face relaxed. A lock of hair rested carelessly on his forehead. The hand on her breast tightened and the nipple was caught between two strong fingers.

Carol gasped and looked again at Simon's sleeping face. A telltale nerve twitched at the corner of his mouth. "You're faking, Simon," she said severely. "You're not asleep!"

A slow smile curved his lips and his eyes opened just far enough for her to see the aroused glint there. "Fooled you, didn't I?" he said huskily.

"Oh, you sap!" She laughed and turned full into his embrace. A three-day growth of beard scratched her soft skin as she nuzzled against him, but she didn't care. He was already beginning to work his magic on her once again with those wonderful hard caressing hands.

"Simon!" she moaned as those hands became more seeking. He was everything she had thought he would be as a lover—and more! In their three days together he had dispelled forever any fears that might have lingered that she was less than a completely sensual woman.

A half hour later they rested in each other's arms, fulfilled and content. "Shall we flip to see who gets up and turns on the heaters?" Simon teased. Power had been restored on the second day, but three feet of shifting snow had kept them captive in their splendid isolation.

"It's your turn," Carol murmured lazily.

"I've noticed that it's my turn every morning," Simon grumbled good-naturedly.

"Just my excuse to see that backside you're so famous for," Carol explained, giving his rear a playful smack.

"Ouch! You'll pay for that one!" Carol giggled as he captured her truant hand and nibbled gently on the tips of her fingers.

"Simon! Come in, please. Over!" The radio set in the corner crackled and they both jumped. This was the first time during their three-day stay that the outside world had impinged on their private haven.

"Come in, please! Over!" Ada's voice repeated.

As Simon wrapped a blanket around himself and went to answer the radio call Carol lay back, the quilts tucked tightly around her. But now she felt cold, not just from Simon's absence but from the sinking feeling that this was the end of the idyll. The time had come to return to reality and the prospect was depressing. For never once—not at the height of rapture nor in the satiated afterglow of their lovemaking—had any word of permanence crossed Simon's lips.

She sighed. Their physical union had deepened and strengthened her love for Simon, and while she knew that he had rejoiced in their lovemaking with an enthusiastic male abandon, the same old doubts still haunted her.

Simon was frowning when he returned to the warmth of the bed. "I have a visitor," he said tersely. "We've got to go back. Sam will be here with the snowmobile in a few minutes."

"Snowmobile! You—you mean that we could have gone . . ."

Simon's ironic smile banished the frown. "Of course. The morning after the storm." He ran a lazy finger down her throat to the hollow between her breasts. "Three days alone with you was too good an opportunity to pass up. You're not sorry we stayed, are you?"

She took so long in answering that his frown returned. "Well?" he asked sharply.

"Nooo," she began hesitantly, badly troubled, "but . . ."

"But what?"

"Simon, I've missed three days working with Katie while we've been here. This is a crucial time for her. I feel it. How can I justify taking my own pleasure at her expense?"

"So you would rather have been with Katie, working, than here with me?"

"I didn't say that, Simon!" she replied impatiently. "I'm saying that my first responsibility is to Katie and her well-being."

"And you feel no responsibility to me, is that it? You resent the fact that I've kept you away from your work?" Anger had tightened his lips and deepened the lines around his mouth.

"Perhaps what I resent is the fact that you didn't even give me a choice!" Her anger was beginning to match his. "You deliberately let me believe that we were stranded here instead of telling me the truth and letting me make the decision as to whether or not Katie's needs had to come first! Why did you do that, Simon?"

"Why?" He laughed, a short harsh sound. "Fool that I was, I thought I meant something to you!"

"Simon!" she exclaimed in exasperation. "You obviously don't understand how I feel."

"No, frankly, I don't. So let's just drop it, shall we?"

Carol was more than ready to let the matter rest. She was deeply troubled by what Simon had said and done. His attitude showed so little appreciation and understanding of the commitment she felt to her profession, a commitment that deeply concerned his own daughter!

As they hurriedly prepared for Sam's arrival the constraint between them grew. Never had she felt so alienated from him, and from Simon's abrupt movements and set expression she knew that he was as disturbed as she. The heavy silence began to etch itself upon her nerves until she could no longer endure it.

"Who is your visitor?" she asked at last in an effort to relieve some of the tension. A sudden premonition of trouble brought a chill to her heart. "Not Madge!"

"No, not Madge. At least, not yet. It's Len Higgenbotham, the county sheriff."

Her hands paused in the act of fastening her coat. "The sheriff! What on earth does he want?"

"I'll find out soon enough without looking for trouble," Simon replied curtly. He paused a moment, a thoughtful expression in his eyes. "Carol, when we get to the house I want you to go upstairs and stay there with Katie until I tell you differently."

"But, Simon—"

"Just do as I ask, please. I know what's best."

The return trip was made in silence, and Carol couldn't even enjoy the pristine beauty of the snow that covered trees and ground. Despite the tension between them, however, their arrival at the castle was like a homecoming for Carol. Still, she felt a sharp twinge of guilt at her first sight of Katie's white, strained face. The child had obviously been hovering anxiously near the door and as soon as they approached she threw herself at Carol and gave her a shuddering, convulsive hug that threatened to choke her.

The combination of warmth and desperation in that little body brought tears to Carol's eyes. She could see at a glance that Katie had had three very bad days. Was that why Ada's welcome was so restrained and edged with more than a hint of hostility? Or did the older woman disapprove of the new, intimate relationship between Simon and herself?

"Len is waiting for you in the study, Simon," the housekeeper said curtly, without preliminaries.

"Take Katie upstairs, Carol."

As Simon disappeared down the hallway to see the sheriff Carol led Katie up to her bedroom. The child was apparently terrified to let Carol out of her sight for fear of losing her again, and the tight grip she had on Carol's hand almost reached the point of pain.

"Katie, darling," she said gently when the girl released her hold only to grab onto Carol's skirt, "how am I going to get out of this dress if you're holding on?"

Reluctantly Katie let go, but to ease her mind Carol allowed her to stay while she repaired the ravages of the last three days. A half hour later, bathed, shampooed and changed, Carol sat with Katie in the playroom, reading her a book. Try as she might, however, she could not keep her thoughts on the plight of three mischievous rabbits—not when a real drama was being enacted downstairs.

What did the sheriff want? she kept asking herself. And why had Simon sent her upstairs?

Fortunately for her nerves, Ada soon interrupted her troubled thoughts.

"Carol, Simon would like to see you in the study. Immediately!"

Carol frowned, disturbed by the grim set of the woman's lips and the hostility in the tone. "What's going on, Ada?"

"Would you just go down, please?" the woman replied curtly.

Anxiously Carol searched Ada's face for some clue, but all she could read there was that something was *very* wrong.

"Is Madge making trouble?" Carol persisted.

"I think it would be better if Simon explained," was all the woman would say. Without another

word she turned on her heel and left a very
worried Carol behind her.

Absently Carol tucked her blouse more firmly
into her jeans and ran a perfunctory hand over
her hair. If the problem was indeed Madge, then
Ada was right to blame her. The trouble in Bar
Harbor had been her fault and Carol was stricken
with remorse.

"Katie," she said, avoiding the child's curious
stare, "I have to see your father for a few
minutes. You stay up here and look at the pictures. I'll be back soon."

Carol tried to smile, but it was a poor thing of
its kind, and she knew that Katie's eyes followed
her anxiously out the door.

Simon was alone when Carol entered the large
paneled study. He sat in a leather chair, his face
grim and set, his eyes far away in thought. He
gave no answering smile to her tentative greeting.
In fact, it took him a moment to notice that she
was even in the room.

"I'm sorry," he said stiffly. "I didn't hear you
come in."

"Simon, what's wrong? Madge?"

In answer he held out a folded paper for her
inspection. "Here. You can read this for yourself."

Slowly Carol unfolded the legal document. She
had never seen one before, but she recognized its
significance at a glance. It was a subpoena. Madge
was taking Simon to court for custody of Katie!

"Oh, Simon!" she whispered inadequately.

He rose and took a quick turn around the

room. "We should have expected it, of course," he said bitterly.

Anxiously her eyes sought his. "It's all my fault, isn't it? She's doing this because of what I said to Rick in Bar Harbor."

His eyes on hers were steady. "I won't try to deceive you, Carol. I just finished talking to my lawyer. Yes, she is using that as the grounds for a new hearing. I told you before that she delights in character assassination. She's claiming that you are both negligent and incompetent, and that my sole concern in bringing you here was for myself and not for Katie's welfare."

Put in such blunt terms, it sounded so . . . so sordid!

"I have worse to tell you," Simon continued before she could speak. "Len has a subpoena to serve on you. Madge is going to drag you into court, too. "

"You suspected this, didn't you?" Her voice was low and heavy with remorse. "That's why you sent me upstairs."

"Yes. I don't want you involved in this. This is my fight, not yours."

Carol shook her head at him in amazement. "Not my fight? What do you mean? I'm right smack in the middle of it all!"

"You aren't going to be," he returned harshly. "I've had my personal life dragged through the mud once. I won't have it again."

"But, Simon," she asked in exasperation, "what can you do? You have no choice!"

"Oh, yes, I do. Madge and her lawyer will be here this afternoon at three. They're bringing

Arthur and a child welfare officer from Bangor. Madge is determined to take Katie away with her." A shudder of pain went through him. "Well, I'll let Katie go. I'll tell Madge to drop the suit and she can keep Katie!"

Carol stared at him incredulously. "Simon! You can't! You can't let Madge have her!"

Simon ran angry fingers through his already disordered hair. "I have no choice! Can't you see that this is the only way I have of protecting you?"

"Protecting *me!*"

"Yes, *you*. Do you want our affair—and now it *is* an affair—making headlines in all the papers? Do you want your professional reputation, your integrity, put on the witness stand for cross-examination? I've been through that before, Carol. I know what it's like. You could never endure the kind of questioning Madge's lawyer would subject you to."

"Simon, please!"

In one swift movement he was beside her, clutching her shoulders with unconsciously hurting hands. "No, listen to me, Carol. I know what's best. I'll let Katie go to Madge. That won't keep Madge quiet entirely, but at least you won't have to go through the indignity of an open court case. We'll go away somewhere—together. Italy or the Caribbean. When it all blows over, we'll come back here. Madge doesn't really want Katie, she just wants the money. I'll strike a deal with her when she's had time to calm down. Katie will be back in the end."

A growing anger held Carol silent and Simon took this silence for agreement.

"You'll go back to Boston," he continued with an assurance that made her want to hit him, "and I'll join you there at the end of the week. Then we can decide where we want to go—"

"Simon!" she interrupted, no longer able to conceal her indignation.

"Please, Carol. There's no time for discussion now. You have to leave before Madge gets here."

"I'm not going anywhere, Simon!"

"You don't understand, Carol," he protested impatiently. "If you're here the child-welfare officer will ask you questions about our relationship. He'll challenge your competence, accuse you of neglect—"

"And you think I can't answer those questions?" Carol was so angry that she was shaking. "Simon, do you think I've done a bad job with Katie? Do you think I've been negligent?"

"No, no! Of course not! But I'm no expert. I have no credibility where Madge is concerned. All I know is that I want you out of here before they come. I won't stand back and watch while that woman humiliates you!"

"I'm not leaving, Simon!"

They stood facing each other, Carol furious with Simon and he seething with frustrated rage at Carol's stubbornness and the impossible position his mother-in-law had put him in.

"I say you're leaving!" he shouted. "Now go upstairs and pack. I'll call Sam and tell him to have the boat in half an hour. I want you gone, off the island—"

"Ahhhhhhh!"

Simon and Carol turned simultaneously. In the

open doorway stood Katie, her face white, her eyes wide and staring.

"Caarrroll!" The sound pierced the silence.

"Katie!" Carol gasped, and Simon echoed the cry.

"Katie!"

"Carol!" the child repeated, the name clear and distinct this time. Then, before either Simon or Carol could reach her, the tension in her snapped and she dropped to the floor in a dead faint.

In one swift movement Simon swooped her up in his arms and cradled her against his body. "I'll take her up to her room."

Moments later, when he had laid her gently on her bed, tears stung his eyes as they met Carol's over his child's head.

"She spoke!" he whispered, his voice choked with emotion.

"Yes, Simon," Carol said, tenderly smoothing Katie's hair back from her face.

"She spoke!" he repeated, the full realization beginning to reach his consciousness.

"Yes." A half-sad, half-ironic smile played lightly over her lips. "This is your miracle, Simon. You can't let Madge take Katie away from you now."

Their attention returned to Katie as she stirred and a low moan came from between her lips. Slowly her eyes opened. First they focused on her father and then searched for Carol.

"Leaving!" she whispered on a sob.

Carol immediately understood the child's fear and she took Katie's hand and raised it to her

cheek. "No, no, darling. I'm staying right here
with you." Her eyes dared Simon to contradict
her.

Katie looked to her father. "Carol . . . leaving?"

For a moment tension held Simon rigid; then
slowly he relaxed and a beautiful smile broke over
his face. "No, Katie. Carol's staying."

Carol remained alone beside Katie's bed while
the child fell into a natural sleep of emotional
exhaustion. As she watched the sleeping girl her
body was motionless, but her mind was racing.
With a deliberate act of will she pushed aside the
personal implications of the day's dramatic events
and concentrated on the professional. As she had
told Simon, Katie's recovery had been little short
of a miracle. She had enough experience in her
profession not to undervalue the possibility of a
miracle, but in Katie's case she was as positive as
she could be that something more tangible than
divine intervention had brought about the cure—
not a complete cure, of course, but at least the
first major step. A full recovery could well de-
pend on Carol's discovering what had happened
to trigger Katie's reaction.

One by one Carol sorted through the facts,
added educated conjectures and sought to form a
picture of the events leading up to her entrance in
the study.

Katie must have been worried about Carol's
long absence and gone in search of her. She must
have overheard at least the last part of her
conversation with Simon. His final words had

probably caused her frantic response. What had they been? She closed her eyes and sought to visualize the moment.

Simon had told her to go upstairs and pack while he called Sam to get the boat ready. She was to leave the island—!

Just as Katie's mother had been about to leave!

Large pieces of the puzzle began to fall into place. The sequence of events the day of Angela's death held the key, she was sure. Simon's words when he told her of that fatal day were clear in her mind. Angela was packing to go. She and Simon quarreled about Katie. Simon went downstairs to call Sam. Angela followed. She fell. Ada and Simon heard the sounds of the fall and went into the hall. Katie was there. . . . Katie was already there!

Where had she come from? Knowing, as she now did, the pattern of Katie's days, the obvious answer was from upstairs. Simon had said that he and Angela hadn't been living together for years before her death. Which room had she slept in? Carol didn't want to ask Simon. First she wanted to make sure about her theory. Ada would know.

Ada was in the kitchen when Carol found her, her head bent over the household accounts. "Ada!" Carol said sharply. She had no patience right now with the woman's antagonism, no matter how justified she might be in blaming Carol for their present dilemma. She was fighting now for both her own professional reputation and Katie's future.

"Ada, which room did Angela use just before her death?"

"Wh-what?" the woman sputtered.

"I said, which room did Angela use just before she died? I know she wasn't sleeping with Simon."

"Why do you want to know?" Ada asked suspiciously.

"Please, Ada! You want to help Katie, don't you? Just tell me!"

"She used the room next to Katie's—your room."

Carol paused for a minute and drew a deep breath. The room next to Katie's! She was almost afraid to ask the next question.

"Think, Ada. This is important. Where was Katie the afternoon her mother was killed? Was she upstairs? And who was with her?"

For a moment Carol was afraid that Ada would refuse to answer, but then she saw that something in her own intense determination had penetrated the hostile barrier. Gradually the woman's face softened.

"You really care, don't you?" she murmured.

"Yes, Ada. I care. I care more than I can tell you," Carol answered solemnly. "Tell me. Where was Katie?"

"The accident happened during her rest time. Amy had put her down for a nap, oh, maybe an hour before."

Carol felt a thrill of elation. The answer was so simple, but then, Simon hadn't known that Katie was just next door when he and Angela had been fighting, and Ada hadn't known about the quarrel!

Katie must have been awakened by their

voices, Carol concluded grimly, and she had heard enough to know that her mother was leaving. What Katie had heard this afternoon in the study had been a repetition of that disastrous day—or fairly close—only this time it was Carol who was to go away.

"What's this all about, Carol?" Ada asked in bewilderment.

"I'm not entirely sure," Carol said slowly, "but I think I'm beginning to understand at last."

Carol was still deep in thought when she left a confused, unsatisfied Ada behind. The hallway was cold and she shivered slightly. At the bottom of the long flight of stone steps leading to the second floor she stood and sought to recreate the scene of a year before. She looked back over her shoulder at the arched doorway leading to the kitchen area. The radio was in a separate room just off the pantry. Simon had been in there calling Sam. Ada had been in the kitchen. It wouldn't have taken them more than a minute to come from the back of the house to the front stairs.

Just about as long as it would have taken Katie to come down the steps!

Simon believed that Katie had rejected him because the child thought he had in some way been responsible for her mother's fall. That could not be true! Katie had to have known that her father was nowhere near the stairs when Angela fell. He had been back in the radio room— downstairs! And today Katie had spoken for the first time to try to prevent Carol from leaving.

Slowly Carol began to mount the stairs, but

gradually her pace quickened. Katie was a docile child. In only two instances had she shown violent emotional reactions before today. The first had been toward her father. The second, however, had been even more significant. The doll! Carol had reached the conclusion that Katie's violence toward the doll had been a hostile reaction to her grandmother. Wrong!

Katie was punishing the child, not the adult. Katie was punishing herself!

A great wave of elation swept through her. She had the answers. She was sure now that she understood the cause of Katie's silence.

At five minutes to three the small party arrived by launch from the mainland. Sam had hooked up a horse to the ancient sleigh to transport the visitors from the dock to the castle.

Madge must be very determined to get Katie back as quickly as possible, Carol thought dryly, to brave the aftermath of the storm.

With Madge were Minta and their distinguished lawyer, Clayton Harrison. Smug, self-satisfied smiles rested comfortably on the women's carefully made-up faces. The other stranger with them was Heber Lee from the county welfare office. Carol liked him on sight. His affable downeast country drawl did nothing to detract from the shrewd Yankee gleam in his eye.

And then there was Arthur. Carol had never seen him looking so grim and her heart gave a lurch of regret. She wouldn't have caused him trouble for the world, but one look at his pallor and the heavy lines in his forehead told her that the past few days had been very difficult for him. For a moment she was almost afraid to meet his eyes. Did he really believe the charges Madge had leveled against her? Just as she was beginning to despair their eyes met and locked, and she released the tense breath she had been holding. Arthur might be worried about her, disturbed by Madge Penrod's allegations, but her old friend and colleague's faith in her had never faltered.

"Arthur," she whispered urgently when introductions had been made, "I've got to have a few minutes alone with you before this whole thing begins!"

The doctor's penetrating gaze took in her excitement and the high color in her cheeks, and slowly his body began to relax. For the first time his lips lost their compressed line and curved into a smile.

"And *I* want to talk to *you*," he said wryly. "My dear girl, you have created quite a stir."

"Wait until you hear what I have to say," Carol pleaded, "and then I'll answer any questions you ask."

"Let's go upstairs and talk, and then I need to see Katie."

Simon led the official delegation into the formal drawing room while Arthur accompanied Carol upstairs.

"Arthur, Katie's speaking again," she began without preamble, "and I'm sure I know now what caused the trauma. Listen and see if you don't think this makes sense . . ."

A half hour later Carol and Arthur rejoined the others. The atmosphere in the drawing room was thick with tension.

"Now that Dr. French has returned," Clayton Harrison asked pompously, "do you think we might begin these proceedings? Mrs. Penrod is very anxious to have Katie in her care once again."

I'll just bet she is, Carol thought cynically. She could practically see dollar signs dancing in the woman's eyes.

"As you know, Mr. Forbes," Lee began, "Dr. French and I are here to determine if there is sufficient reason to remove Katie from your care immediately for her own safety or mental well-being. A court will, of course, have to decide on permanent custody, but the issue at hand is whether or not Dr. Durand's alleged professional negligence has had a harmful effect on the child, enough to justify her removal."

"How could a grandmother have any peace of mind," Madge interrupted, "knowing that her sweet grandchild was in that woman's care!"

"We all appreciate your concern," Arthur said dryly. He looked to Simon. "You haven't told her?"

"No. I thought the pleasure of relating that news rightly belonged to Carol."

The two men smiled in warm understanding as heads swiveled to where Carol stood in front of the fireplace.

"What are you two talking about?" Madge demanded.

"Carol?" Arthur prompted.

"Mrs. Penrod," she began, "because you are so concerned, I know that you're going to be delighted to hear that Katie is speaking again." Somehow she managed to keep the irony out of her voice.

"Speaking!" Madge echoed faintly, her face turning a sickly shade of gray. "I—I don't believe it!"

"I talked with her myself just now," Arthur confirmed. "Dr. Durand has accomplished far more than we could ever have hoped for in such a short time. I have nothing but admiration for her expert skill and diligent work."

Every word he spoke was like a blow driving Madge Penrod deeper and deeper into her chair. For a moment her shock prevented her from disputing these statements. Minta, however, filled the gap.

"If Katie is speaking again," she asked insolently, "what makes you think *she* had anything to do with it?"

No one gave the question serious enough consideration to respond. Her own lawyer was looking at her in disgust.

"I think it might be enlightening," Arthur said smoothly, "if Dr. Durand would provide you with some of the details of Katie's problem. Carol?"

"Of course." She looked to Simon. "That is, if Simon will allow me to reveal some information told to me in professional confidence?"

Simon frowned for a moment, then shrugged. "I guess there's no reason why you shouldn't."

Once again Carol addressed the group as a whole. Quickly and emotionlessly she told of the quarrel between Simon and Angela and the cause of it. "So finally," she concluded, "Angela agreed to leave Katie with Simon when she left the island to join her lover."

"I don't believe a word of this!" Madge said faintly, but the gray lines around her mouth spoke for themselves.

"Well, I do!" Minta piped in. "Angela always was a—"

"Araminta!" her mother snapped.

"Er, carry on, Carol," Arthur prompted.

"What Simon and Angela didn't know," she continued as dispassionately as possible, "was that Katie was in the room next door. I don't know how much of the quarrel she overheard, but it must have been enough for her to realize that her mother was leaving her father—and herself. We'll probably never know for sure exactly what happened, but this much we can guess pretty accurately. Simon went downstairs alone to arrange for the boat. When Angela left the bedroom Katie followed her to the stairs. She called out to her mother, in pain and possibly in anger. Angela could have turned too quickly or tripped or simply been startled and lost her balance, but whatever the case, she fell to her death."

"And Katie's voice?" Simon asked, still puzzled.

"Don't you see? Katie believed that her mother's death was all her fault, that by calling out she had caused the fall."

"And that's why she has refused to speak?" Simon asked incredulously.

"Not really refused," Carol corrected. "The loss of her voice wasn't a conscious decision on her part. We know that guilt does terrible things to adults, but often we don't consider that it's equally traumatic for a child who doesn't have the experience or the perception to understand exactly what's wrong."

"Guilt?" Simon frowned. "Because of an accident?"

"Simon," Carol explained patiently, "Katie wasn't just frightened of what had happened. She was guilty because she had been angry with her mother, perhaps in a childish way even wished her harm, so that when the fall occurred she believed she had killed Angela as surely as though she had pushed her down the stairs herself."

For several moments the whole assemblage sat in stunned silence. Madge was the first to rally. "I for one don't believe a word of it," she objected halfheartedly.

No one was prepared to listen to her.

"And you say that Katie is speaking again?" the welfare officer asked.

"Yes," Arthur reaffirmed. "Very hesitantly and a little reluctantly, but her words are definitely audible. This is a fine beginning."

"Well, then," Heber Lee said, smiling, "I don't see that there's anything more to be said."

After less than ten minutes of futile blustering on Madge's part the matter was settled. Carol's reputation had been restored and Madge's lawyer had informed his client in no uncertain terms that a custody suit was out of the question. Simon's world had been made whole. Only Carol was left with the fear that hers was in pieces.

"Good-bye, Arthur, and thank you," Carol said sincerely as she walked him to the door.

"No need to thank me, my dear," he returned, squeezing her hand affectionately. "You did all the work and no one was more relieved than I to have your name cleared. By the way, when do you plan to return to Boston?"

"I'll stay on another week or ten days. That ought to be enough time to help Katie begin sorting herself out. Complete recovery will come with time and Simon's love. I—I don't want her to become too dependent on me now."

Arthur's sharp eyes missed neither her pallor nor her trembling lips. "I sent you up here for a rest cure," he said gruffly, "and now you're looking worse than when you left. Perhaps it will have to be the South Seas cruise after all."

Carol smiled wanly, but she didn't find this a joking matter. Now that her professional problems had been solved the time had come to deal with her personal problems with Simon. Cravenly, she would have put off a confrontation until another day when she felt less exhausted and emotionally drained, but the anger and despair she had carried with her for the past few hours would give her no peace.

Gathering her courage, she sought him out in his study, where he had retreated after Madge and her party had gone. With a nice sense of delicacy he had tactfully withdrawn to give Carol a few minutes alone with Arthur. From the way he was watching the door when she entered, however, she knew that he had been eagerly waiting for her to come.

"Carol, you were wonderful," he said huskily, moving to take her in his arms. But she held him off with a quick shake of her head and a movement away from him. "What is it?" he asked, frowning. "What's the matter?"

"Sit down, Simon, please," she said wearily as she sank into a chair. "You—you know I hate it when you tower over me like that."

Concern darkened his features as he examined her pale, drawn face. For a moment he hesitated by the side of her chair before he took a place opposite her.

"I don't understand, Carol. What can possibly be wrong? You were wonderful today!"

"No," she said, the bitterness in her voice battling with the fatigue—and winning. "You don't understand!"

"What the hell is the matter with you? I thought you would be overjoyed. I thought to-night would be a celebration!"

"*You* gave me a lot to think about earlier this afternoon, and I couldn't find any joy there."

Impatiently he moved to stand, but Carol restrained him with an abrupt gesture.

"Before we go on with this," she continued quickly, "can we finish up with the business of Katie? You're going to have to do a lot of work with her in the next little while, Simon," she hurried on, not waiting for his agreement. "Only the assurance of your love will help complete her healing process."

"Carol," he began, "let's—"

"You understand why she rejected you, don't you?" she interrupted hastily.

With a sigh Simon gave up the attempt to dictate the topic of conversation. "No, actually, I don't. She had to know that I loved her."

"But she believed she had forfeited the right to that love," Carol explained. "She believed she had done something so wicked that if you knew, you wouldn't love her anymore. So she withdrew into her own world."

Simon frowned at this. "But lately she's been better. At times I even saw some of my old Katie back."

"I—I don't know if I can explain it entirely," she faltered. "In some measure it was because time was dulling some of the fears." She hesitated. This next part was going to be much more painful to discuss, but professional honesty drove her on. "But there was something else, too. She saw us together and began to look upon me as a replacement—for want of a better word—for her mother. She began to hope that perhaps the harm she had done hadn't been irreparable. If you could replace the person she had taken from you . . ."

Simon was looking at her sharply. "Well, go on. You were going to say that if I could replace her mother—my *wife*—then perhaps there was hope for her after all?"

"That's right." Carol fervently prayed that she sounded calmer than she felt.

"Then it seems to me," he said slowly, his eyes

never leaving her face, "that what we have to do is make her hopes come true."

"What?" she asked weakly.

"You heard me. Carol, I'm asking you to marry me."

"For Katie's sake?" Try as she might, she couldn't keep the bitterness out of her voice.

"No! Not for Katie's sake. For mine, for yours —for ours!" He rose now and reached down to pull her to her feet, and she didn't prevent him when he kept her hands in his. "Marry me, Carol!"

Absently she looked down at those strong hands that she loved so much. "Do you know, Simon?" she said thoughtfully. "If you had asked me this morning I would have been happier than I've ever been in my life. I would have accepted— and would have made the biggest mistake of my life!"

His hands tightened on hers and she looked up in time to see the fleeting pain in his eyes. "You don't really mean that, do you?"

"Believe me, Simon, I do! Today you suggested without a moment's thought or hesitation that I turn my back on Katie and on my profession. You had no confidence in my ability to withstand difficult times, to fight for my reputation, to defend an attack on my integrity, to combat Madge. . . ."

"Carol, you were wonderful today when you faced Madge and her lawyer down! I couldn't believe it when in five minutes you explained the trauma that had mystified Arthur—"

"No, I know you could hardly believe it!" she interrupted bitterly. "Do you think I didn't see the look on your face? You couldn't have been more surprised if I had suddenly begun speaking in Hindustani!"

"Perhaps you did surprise me," he agreed, "but believe me when I tell you I love you! Anything I said or did today grew out of that love."

For a moment Carol was shaken by the intensity of his words—the words she had so longed to hear. Then she sadly shook her head.

"No, I can't believe that, Simon. At least, I can't believe you love me in the way I want—need!—to be loved."

"You don't believe I really love you?" he asked harshly.

"I *know* you don't! When I found out that you had had me actually hide from the sheriff, when you virtually ordered me to turn tail and run, I knew that you had no inkling of who or what I am! You showed no concept of what I think or feel or believe in, of what I value and what I reject, of my priorities and goals—"

"That's not true!"

"It is, Simon! If you had had *any* understanding of what makes me what I am you would never have suggested that I be a party to meekly turning Katie over to Madge to save myself trouble or embarrassment. I would have fought tooth and nail, with every ounce of knowledge and energy I had, to save Katie from her grandmother. And I would have prayed that you would have the courage to do the same. I know you were trying to protect me—whether out of mistaken love or personal pride, I don't know. But I would have had a lot more faith in your love if you had shown a little confidence in my strength of character and skill as a doctor."

"Carol!" His voice was filled with pain and, loving him as she did, she shared that pain. "I love you!"

"No, Simon, don't talk to me of love, because I know what I'm talking about. You see, *I love you!* I love you very much."

His hand tightened on hers, and his eyes darkened. "Then . . ."

"No!" she said quickly, pulling her hands free. "Please let me finish. You're a very handsome man, Simon, and perhaps that's what attracted me in the beginning. But just as your profession leads you to look for the physical attributes in a person, mine has trained me to look beneath the surface—just as you feared." Her ironic smile went awry. "Right from the start I saw you as a man of complex emotions and drives. As I came to know you I found vulnerability, humor and intelligence, tenderness and compassion. I grew to love you for your wonderful strengths, but I love you, too, for your weaknesses—your quick temper, your irritability, your cynical view of life."

"Then why won't you marry me?" he asked in honest bewilderment.

"Simon, don't you see? I don't want to be loved and appreciated just because you think I have a—a sexy body, one that you can recreate in bronze! You may love my *outside,* but you don't know anything about what I am *inside!* I want to be loved as a whole person—a thinking, feeling woman—not the hothouse flower you once called me, too weak to withstand a strong wind."

"Carol, I *do* love you," he pleaded. "I swear it!"

"Words are easy, Simon. It's what a person *does* that counts. Perhaps I'm a little cynical myself." She smiled wanly. "Experience taught me some very hard lessons. It took me time to accept the fact that Brian had loved me in his own hollow way, but I knew that he loved my money more. Rick loved me, too—but not as I was. He was always trying to mold and change me into the kind of woman he wanted me to be. You love me in still another way. You chose to see me as Beatrice to your Dante! And, like Dante, you look for some male ideal of what a woman is instead of seeing me as I am."

Slowly Simon absorbed her words—and he no longer protested. A heavy silence hung between them. At last he turned from her to stare out at the bleak snow-covered landscape. It looked no more desolate than Carol felt.

"And nothing I can say now," he asked soberly, thoughtfully, "can make any difference to you, can it?"

Weakly Carol shook her head. "I'm sorry, Simon." Her voice was filled with immeasurable regret.

"And you're going back to Boston now?"

"I'll stay another week and then I have to go."

He turned to her then with a strange expression —not the artist's look, not even the ardent, passionate, tender gaze of the lover she had known. This was something quite, quite different —unfathomable.

"Yes," he said slowly. "I understand."

Carol had won the argument, but it afforded her no satisfaction. She had lost too much with the victory.

"I have something to ask of you, Carol."

"What?" she asked wearily.

"There's been too much between us to let it just end like this. All I ask is that you give me some time—give us both some time—to think things over."

"Oh, Simon!" she cried. "What good will that do? I've been thinking and thinking since the moment I knew I loved you!"

He came near her then to stare down into her upturned face. His bright, magnetic gaze held her transfixed. "Just two months," he said softly. "That's all I ask."

"Two months?" she breathed weakly.

"Two months weighed against a lifetime, Carol. Is that too much to ask?"

"But why? For what?" Her words pleaded for understanding, for hope.

Gently he drew her into his arms. "You'll see."

His lips on hers were soft and undemanding, but she sensed his desperation and could not for the life of her deny his request.

"All right, Simon. Two months, and then we'll talk again."

Chapter Eleven

"I simply can't imagine what you're doing going out on a night like this," Cora chided as Carol pulled on her heavy fur-lined gloves. "This weather isn't fit for man or beast. I don't remember a January like it."

Somehow her aunt managed to imply that it was all Carol's fault. But then, everything that had gone wrong in the past two months had somehow been Carol's fault. Rick had become engaged to a young debutante of eighteen and his break with Carol had caused a good deal of unpleasant speculation. Good old Rick, it seemed, had maintained his own pride at the expense of Carol's reputation.

"Here! You've forgotten your scarf!" Cora tutted as she followed Carol to the door.

"Thank you, Cora," Carol said absently, winding the wool scarf around her neck.

Outside she shivered in spite of her heavy fur coat and ducked her head to avoid the biting wind. Ten straight days of subzero temperatures after one of the worst blizzards in years had nearly crippled the city. Traffic crawled, schools were closed and the sidewalks were deserted. This was without a doubt the worst January of her life—for more reasons than the weather, she concluded morosely.

She hadn't heard a word from Simon. She hadn't really known what to expect when she left Maine, but it hadn't been this silence. In her heart she wanted to believe that he had left her alone to avoid putting undue pressure on her. But he could at least have sent a postcard!

He had asked her to think things over, but it seemed that he was the one who had had second thoughts! For herself, she was incapable of putting him out of her mind. During the day she disciplined herself to work and at night spent long hours at the typewriter. But she had no control over her dreams. Each morning she awoke tense and depressed, haunted by the fear that she had forfeited any hope of future happiness for a very cold and lonely principle. Marriage to Simon might never have been the true union of spirits she had dreamed of, but at least she would have been near him, could have touched him, loved him.

Arthur threw open the car door as she approached and she slid quickly inside. "Whew!"

she sighed, leaning back in the leather seat, catching her breath and settling into the welcoming warmth. "Only you, Arthur, would think this a fit night for a dinner date!"

Arthur smiled benignly and eased his large vintage Cadillac out of Carol's drive and into the street. "How's the book coming along?" he asked when he was clear of the ice-covered side street and onto the well-salted main road.

"Fine. It will be ready to go to the typist next week. In fact," she added, "I really ought to be home right now finishing the rewrites."

"Nonsense!" he said heartily. "You'll be better for the break. You can only beat a willing horse so long, my dear, and you're pushing yourself too hard again! You've been wandering around the clinic like a wraith these past few weeks. Some good food, a bottle or two of expensive wine, a little witty conversation with a relaxing companion. Just what the doctor ordered."

His warm coaxing tone allayed her suspicions, but not entirely. She had no reason to believe that he wasn't concerned about her and desirous of giving her a relaxing evening, but he had been behaving very peculiarly the past few days. He had been whistling around the office with that cat-that-caught-the-canary smile he had when he was up to something.

"Just where are we going, Arthur?"

"A new French restaurant I've discovered. Veal cordon bleu that melts in your mouth!"

Carol smiled at his enthusiasm and relaxed. She knew that the one vice he allowed himself was pampering his gourmet's palate with the best in food and fine wine. For the rest of the short drive into the heart of the city they sat in companionable silence. Actually, Carol was happy to be out for a change. She was becoming much too introspective for her own good.

The restaurant was all that Arthur had promised. The atmosphere was one of subdued elegance, the food was cooked to perfection and the wine list included a number of rare vintages that made Arthur's eyes sparkle. Try as she might, however, she could not do justice to the beef and mushroom concoction that Arthur had ordered for her, and she drank only sparingly of the Saint-Émilion claret, 1959, that accompanied the meal.

Arthur watched her push her food around on her plate until his finer instincts were outraged. "I should have taken you out for a hamburger and fries," he grumbled.

"I'm sorry, Arthur," she apologized sincerely. "I—I just don't seem to have any appetite lately."

Not until the coffee came did he bring up the subject she had been dreading. "What have you heard from Katie lately?"

"She's doing fine," she said with a false cheerfulness. "S-Simon took her to Florida after Christmas for a few days to let her get some sun." It annoyed her that she stumbled over Simon's name. "She sent me some pictures of herself playing in the ocean."

She didn't add that Katie had slipped in one of her father, also, and that she had lost a night's sleep thinking of Simon's lean, tanned body in a brief blue bathing suit lounging on the beach.

Who had taken the picture? she had wondered, experiencing her first pangs of jealousy.

Abruptly Arthur checked his watch. "Time to go."

Carol looked at her half-finished cup of coffee and shrugged. She had no desire to prolong the conversation, goodness knew!

Once in the car again, Carol leaned back and closed her eyes. The evening certainly couldn't be considered a success. She knew her conversation had been stilted and she hadn't been able to shake the faint tension she felt. Was it reaching the point where she wasn't fit company for anyone, even an old friend like Arthur?

They had been driving for nearly ten minutes before she realized that Arthur was going in the opposite direction from her home. "Where are we?" she asked in bewilderment.

"Oh, I just have one stop to make," he said casually. "I didn't think you would mind."

"No, no. Of course I don't." She settled back into the seat, her gaze focused on the passing street lights and shop windows, her thoughts a mixture of unrelated impressions and feelings. Her wandering attention was soon recalled, however, when Arthur turned off Beacon Street and pulled into a parking space.

"What are we doing here?" she asked sharply. Her eyes were fixed on the large brass doors of the art gallery. She had not been there since the October night when she had first met Simon.

"Oh, there's a particular piece I need to see," he said casually.

"But the gallery is closed," she said, stating the

obvious. The gallery was dark except for security lights.

"I talked with the owner earlier in the day. He said he would be glad to let us in for a few minutes. They've been setting up a new exhibit for tomorrow."

"Then why not wait until tomorrow?" she asked practically.

He turned and smiled his most winning, disarming smile. "Because I want your opinion of it and you're always too busy!"

Carol studied his face for a moment in the dim light, but his expression was bland and she shrugged philosophically. After all, Arthur didn't know that if he had planned a torture especially for her, he couldn't have chosen anything worse than bringing her here. Her memories of that first encounter with Simon were still far too vivid. Had her love for him been sparked at that first moment? she wondered with a pain that twisted in her heart.

"All right?" Arthur asked, his eyes studying her face intently.

Oh, well, she thought stoically. At least Simon's exhibit was long gone, and she was going to have to learn to endure these periodic reminders. "Sure," she said. "Let's go."

The guard must have been watching for them. He opened the door at the first sound of Arthur's knock. "Not a good night to be out, sir," he said cheerfully as he helped Carol off with her coat and hung it on the rack.

"Wind's dying down a little," Arthur returned, removing his own coat.

"You know which room?"

"Yes, thank you."

"Light switch is just to the right of the door."
With that he went back to the small lighted office
near the entrance.

Their footsteps echoed loudly in the empty
room as they crossed the main exhibit hall. The
coming showing was the work of a modern abstract sculptor and the welded metal shapes
looked grotesque in the dim light. Carol couldn't
suppress a shiver. She felt a little like a ghost of
her former self haunting a familiar path from her
unhappy past.

"Where are we going?" she asked to dispel the
mood and her voice echoed back at her.

"Just through here," Arthur said, taking her
arm and directing her through a broad arched
doorway to a smaller room beyond. "Go on in
and I'll find the light."

Her eyes had adapted to the darkness and she
blinked as the fluorescent ceiling lights stuttered
into brilliant life. She had time only to note that
Arthur was watching her intently when all coher-
ent thought was driven from her head.

In front of her on a raised platform was the
statue of a woman resting on a large base. One
look told her whose work it was. She would
recognize Simon's distinctive style anywhere. This
statue, however, was not of a nude. The figure
was clothed in a flowing gown and covering outer
robe. She sat with her legs tucked beneath her,
reclining on one hand. The other hand toyed with
a strand of long hair that hung over her shoulder.
Carol only noticed this in passing. What drew her

attention and brought a startled gasp from between her parted lips was the face of the woman. It was her own face that stared pensively out at her from beneath half-shuttered eyes!

Carol's eyes flew to the title card propped against the base. It read simply: "Carol."

Unconsciously Carol stepped nearer. Now she even recognized the clothing. It was the negligee and peignoir she had worn the evening Simon had come to her room, the night he had first suggested that she model for him!

Her gaze was drawn in fascination back to the face. Had she ever really looked like that? She could hardly believe that this was the way Simon saw her! The expression on the statue's face was a combination of humor and thoughtfulness, but still there was a sensuality in the reclining languor of the figure and the smile on the slightly parted lips. This was no virgin goddess, no artist's abstract ideal. This was a living, breathing modern woman—complex and enigmatic.

"I hope you like it," said a voice from behind her—and she froze.

There was no mistaking that deep husky voice, no mistaking the rich timbre that had the power to turn her limbs to water. Only one man had a voice like that. She closed her eyes and breathed deeply to calm her frantic heart. Oh, if only her legs would stop shaking!

"Well? Don't you have anything to say?"

The voice was deeper still, but Carol didn't miss the note of anxiety. Slowly she turned to face him. He stood in the doorway, his hands thrust negligently into the pockets of his leather jacket, but she saw at once that his air of ease was assumed. The muscles in his throat tightened as he forced a smile to his lips.

"Simon," she breathed. For the life of her, she was unable to say anything more.

Slowly he closed the distance between them. "You're too thin," he said harshly.

"You—you've lost weight yourself."

For a long moment they just stared at each other. Suddenly Carol was aware that they were alone.

"Where did Arthur go?"

"Home."

"Home?" she repeated vaguely.

"He knew you would be safe with me."

"Safe?" she murmured dumbly.

"The two months are nearly up, Carol," he informed her soberly.

"The two months," she repeated, raising a cold and shaking hand to her heated cheek. Was she doomed to echo him so inanely when there was so much she longed to say, so much she wanted to know, so many questions she had to ask? She felt as though she was bungling her whole future!

"You haven't told me how you like your statue."

"It—it isn't Beatrice," she whispered.

"No, it isn't Beatrice. It's you."

Their eyes met again and what Carol read in his set her pulse racing.

"Well, do you like it?" he persisted. For the first time a hint of irritation showed through his anxiety—and she wanted to kiss him! Oh, this was the Simon she loved so dearly! Abrupt and irritable when he was frustrated or anxious. But she didn't know how to answer him. She still found it difficult to believe all that his statue of her implied.

"I haven't heard a word from you in two months," she offered instead.

"You told me that words were easy, that it was what a man *did* that counted with you."

She couldn't resist the impulse to reach out her trembling hand and lay it against his lean cheek. "You—you did this statue for me?"

He turned his head and pressed a kiss into her palm. "How else could I show you what you mean to me?"

"Oh, Simon!"

Suddenly she was in his arms and she gave herself up thankfully to his embrace. It was like being invited home again after a long, lonely exile. Tears of thanksgiving rolled down her cheeks and mingled with the warm moisture of their mouths.

"Please," Simon murmured, "don't cry!"

"I'm just so happy! I thought I had lost you forever!"

"And I thought I had offended you beyond all forgiveness. Only when I saw your face when you looked at the statue did I begin to hope. I've been living in agony these past weeks, terrified that nothing I could do could make any difference!"

"Oh! I'm so sorry, Simon!"

"No, you have nothing to apologize for! I was the one who was a fool—a stupid, blind fool! Everything you said to me that afternoon was the truth. My only excuse is that I had never known a woman like you, Carol. My experience with Angela did little for my faith in women. My judgment became warped. And I've always considered myself such an enlightened man!" His arms tightened around her and she read the chagrin in his eyes.

"Forget it, Simon. Please."

"If you can forgive me I'm not sure I want to forget it." He smiled ruefully. "I regret the pain I caused you, but I can't regret the lesson I learned."

"What was that?" Her voice was soft and gently she rubbed the back of his neck to ease the tension there.

"Loving you has been a very humbling experience, my darling. I think I must have loved you from the first moment I saw you, but I only admitted it to myself the day I thought you were lost in the storm. You'll never know the terror in my heart as I searched for you. To find you safe was an incredible, blessed relief! But eight years of a loveless marriage had left some deep wounds and I think I was afraid to examine my love for you too deeply for fear I would find it an illusion. I just accepted the fact that at that moment I wanted you and needed you desperately."

"Didn't you know then that I loved you?" she asked softly.

"I hoped, of course, but I didn't really know until you told me that afternoon—and told me *why* you loved me. You made me ashamed of the shallow love I had offered you."

"Oh, Simon!" She pressed herself against him

to soften the pain she read in his eyes at the memory.

"As an artist I had studied all the great lovers of history, Carol, but it took you to teach me what love really is! What hurt the worst was when you said that my profession had taught me to look only at the surface. That was a very humbling moment for me, my love. Any artist with any pretense to greatness believes that what he is trying to capture in a work of art is the *soul* of his subject. That was the moment I vowed to do this statue—to show you the lesson I had learned and prove something to myself."

"Is that how you really see me, Simon?"

"No artist could really do you justice, Carol. I plan on a lifetime to explore all the warm, wonderful intricacies of the woman I love. Will you marry me?"

Her kiss answered for her. Her lips melted onto his with the heat of her love and two lonely months of longing. As footsteps echoed down the hall toward them their bodies drew apart but their eyes joined them.

"Everything all right, Mr. Forbes?" the guard asked.

"Everything is fine, Jensen. Absolutely perfect! Well, almost perfect," he amended as the guard's footsteps faded into the distance. "Will you stay with me tonight?"

Carol felt the familiar weakness invade her limbs at the sight of the smoldering fire in his eyes. "That—that sounds like . . . heaven!" she breathed.

"We'll spend the night looking for it together!"

"Let me just have one more look at the statue," she asked and they both turned. Had any woman ever had such a tribute? she wondered in awe.

"A labor of love," Simon said simply.

For just a moment Carol's glance rested on the softly parted bronze lips and she could have sworn that the smile there was just a little warmer, just a little more knowing, than it had been before.

Outside Simon's apartment in Brookline a frozen world slept on, but inside Carol snuggled contentedly against Simon's warm body.

"Have I ever told you," she said dreamily, "that what I first loved about you were your hands?"

"My hands?" he murmured against the soft skin of her shoulder.

"Yes, you have the largest thumbs!"

"Why, so I do," he said in some surprise, and immediately put them to good use teasing and tantalizing the hard peak of her breast. With a gasp Carol buried her face against his shoulder, exposing her ear to his seeking mouth. His tongue traced the soft lobe and then began to explore each hollow and crevice. Carol was not idle. Daintily her lips nibbled on the hard cords of his neck, working their way up until they rested against the spot where his pulse throbbed.

"You taste good," she breathed in contentment. "A little like—like salted shrimp!"

She smiled as he rose up and looked at her—one blue eye meeting one brown eye.

"In fact, from this angle you look a little like a shrimp!"

"You'll pay for that one, woman!"

"All right," she amended. "A crab." Her reward was a light pinch on the rear. "Oww!" she protested.

"Here," Simon said with questionable solicitude. "I'll rub it better!"

His touch was light, but it took little to stir the fires that smoldered just below the surface. His mouth sought hers and once again she knew the exquisite delight of the touch of his hands. Just as he worked his clay he kneaded each inch of her soft flesh with a sureness and rhythm that set every nerve atingle. And his thumbs! she thought, while she could still think at all. He was exploring her body with a thoroughness that kept her breathless and searching helplessly for the relief that only he could bring.

Their union when it came was swift and fierce—an explosion of sensations that fused their bodies. Slowly Carol drifted down from the heights of pleasure to the cradled valley of contentment.

"Desired in *love*, my darling," Simon murmured, and she knew from the huskiness in his voice and dampness of his cheek against hers that the word had taken on an even deeper, richer meaning for both of them. Their quest was over.

MORE ROMANCE FOR
A SPECIAL WAY TO RELAX

$1.95 each

2 ☐ Hastings	21 ☐ Hastings	41 ☐ Halston	60 ☐ Thorne
3 ☐ Dixon	22 ☐ Howard	42 ☐ Drummond	61 ☐ Beckman
4 ☐ Vitek	23 ☐ Charles	43 ☐ Shaw	62 ☐ Bright
5 ☐ Converse	24 ☐ Dixon	44 ☐ Eden	63 ☐ Wallace
6 ☐ Douglass	25 ☐ Hardy	45 ☐ Charles	64 ☐ Converse
7 ☐ Stanford	26 ☐ Scott	46 ☐ Howard	65 ☐ Cates
8 ☐ Halston	27 ☐ Wisdom	47 ☐ Stephens	66 ☐ Mikels
9 ☐ Baxter	28 ☐ Ripy	48 ☐ Ferrell	67 ☐ Shaw
10 ☐ Thiels	29 ☐ Bergen	49 ☐ Hastings	68 ☐ Sinclair
11 ☐ Thornton	30 ☐ Stephens	50 ☐ Browning	69 ☐ Dalton
12 ☐ Sinclair	31 ☐ Baxter	51 ☐ Trent	70 ☐ Clare
13 ☐ Beckman	32 ☐ Douglass	52 ☐ Sinclair	71 ☐ Skillern
14 ☐ Keene	33 ☐ Palmer	53 ☐ Thomas	72 ☐ Belmont
15 ☐ James	35 ☐ James	54 ☐ Hohl	73 ☐ Taylor
16 ☐ Carr	36 ☐ Dailey	55 ☐ Stanford	74 ☐ Wisdom
17 ☐ John	37 ☐ Stanford	56 ☐ Wallace	75 ☐ John
18 ☐ Hamilton	38 ☐ John	57 ☐ Thornton	76 ☐ Ripy
19 ☐ Shaw	39 ☐ Milan	58 ☐ Douglass	77 ☐ Bergen
20 ☐ Musgrave	40 ☐ Converse	59 ☐ Roberts	78 ☐ Gladstone

Silhouette Special Edition

MORE ROMANCE FOR
A SPECIAL WAY TO RELAX

$2.25 each

79 ☐ Hastings	85 ☐ Beckman	91 ☐ Stanford	97 ☐ Shaw
80 ☐ Douglass	86 ☐ Halston	92 ☐ Hamilton	98 ☐ Hurley
81 ☐ Thornton	87 ☐ Dixon	93 ☐ Lacey	99 ☐ Dixon
82 ☐ McKenna	88 ☐ Saxon	94 ☐ Barrie	100 ☐ Roberts
83 ☐ Major	89 ☐ Meriwether	95 ☐ Doyle	101 ☐ Bergen
84 ☐ Stephens	90 ☐ Justin	96 ☐ Baxter	102 ☐ Wallace

*LOOK FOR THUNDER AT DAWN BY PATTI BECKMAN
AVAILABLE IN AUGUST AND
SUMMER COURSE IN LOVE BY CAROLE HALSTON
IN SEPTEMBER.*

Genuine Silhouette sterling silver bookmark for only $15.95!

What a beautiful way to hold your place in your current romance! This genuine sterling silver bookmark, with the distinctive Silhouette symbol in elegant black, measures 1½" long and 1" wide. It makes a beautiful gift for yourself, and for every romantic you know! And, at only $15.95 each, including all postage and handling charges, you'll want to order several now, while supplies last.

Send your name and address with check or money order for $15.95 per bookmark ordered to

**Simon & Schuster Enterprises
120 Brighton Rd., P.O. Box 5020
Clifton, N.J. 07012
Attn: Bookmark**

Bookmarks can be ordered pre-paid only. No charges will be accepted. Please allow 4-6 weeks for delivery.

N.Y. State Residents
Please Add Sales Tax